THE AMBLE BRANCH

Bartle Rippon

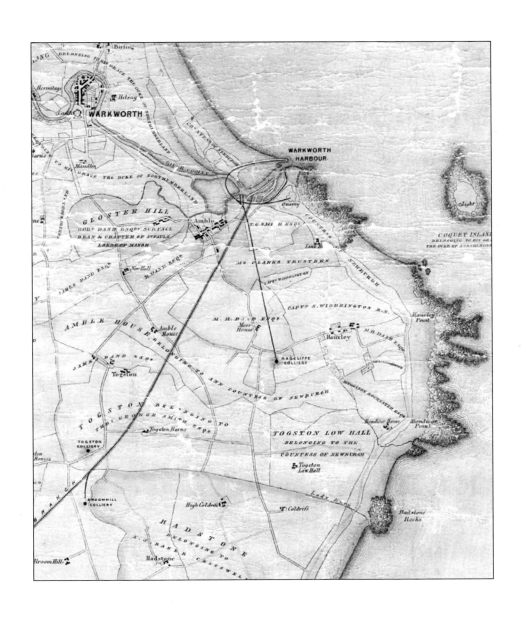

Kestrel Railway Books
PO Box 269
SOUTHAMPTON
SO30 4XR

www.kestrelrailwaybooks.co.uk

Printed by The Amadeus Press

ISBN 978-1-905505-05-0

Front cover: *Darlington's class 4MT 43057 stands proudly at the head of the RCTS/SLS North Eastern Tour – the last passenger train to visit Amble. The train is being reversed into the station platform prior to its departure on a rather sunny Sunday 29th September 1963. The occasion is being carefully observed by the photographers enjoying the spectacular view from one of the NER signal gantries that adorned the area. (Ian S Carr)*

Title Page: *A map dating from around 1849 showing the branch line into Amble. As can be seen, Amble was only a small village during this period, although the harbour appears to be well used with the rail link from Radcliffe Colliery. Togston Colliery is also shown, although a rail link was yet to be established to it. The other interesting feature is the railway that ran from the quarry around the harbour and across the river to the north pier. (Northumberland Record Office)*

Back cover: *In around 1970, the evening sun sets, and shadows are cast over the harbour and the staiths. The distant Warkworth castle stands as proud as ever watching the end of an era – coal exports. What fate awaits these gigantic monuments of a once thriving coal industry? Demolition will soon begin and these staiths will disappear into history. (Bartle Rippon)*

Dedication

This book is dedicated to my wife, Judy, for all the support and encouragement
she has given to a devoted railway enthusiast over the years.

Contents

Acknowledgements

My thanks go to the staff at the National Archives at Kew, the Record Offices at Newcastle (Gosforth) and Morpeth, the libraries of Amble and Alnwick, and the Ken Hoole Study Centre, Darlington. All photographic copyright has been extensively sought, and apologies are given for any that have been unsuccessfully located.

Thanks to George Reeve and Martin Smith of Irwell Press who have allowed publication of material from the article *A Ramble to Amble* that appeared in the June 2005 issue of *Railway Bylines*.

Thanks also for advice and information from J Calvert, Ian S Carr, DK Jones, E Simonsen, J Talbot, F Wake, Harry Wilson of Henry Wilson Books and Colin Wood.

The publishers would like to thank Peter Trundell and Roger Hateley for their assistance with the artwork for this book.

Bibliography:
Amble Junction, EE Whyman
Industrial Locomotives of Northumberland, Industrial Railway Society
Lost Railways of Northumberland, Robert Kinghorn
North East Locomotive Sheds, K Hoole
The *Railways of Northumberland* series, CR Warn
Railways of Northumberland, Alan Young
Signals to Danger, JA Wells

Introduction

Much has been written about the railways of Northumberland, whether they were owned by the North Eastern Railway, the London & North Eastern Railway, the North British, the Blyth and Tyne, or were independent, privately-owned colliery and quarry lines. However, one railway line that has escaped detailed written attention is the mineral line from Amble Junction to the mouth of the River Coquet – a mineral line from the East Coast main line, which boasted a passenger service for 50 years of its 120-year life. It was a branch line of some 5 miles over very gentle, undulating land where there were two cuttings, five overbridges, three underbridges, a level crossing and two stations.

I have always been fascinated with my hometown railway line, the more so after watching the trains coast past the end of the Secondary Modern (now the Middle School) playing fields both into and out of Amble. Some of my peers were able to recognise the various types of locomotive, and it seemed much more fun watching the trains than taking notice of what was going on in the classroom!

Having explored this railway line from Amble to the junction with the main line in the summer of 1969, I began to notice its features and what was needed to operate this short branch line. However, I could never find more than a paragraph or two in railway books relating to the railway to Amble, so the lack of written information prompted me to research the history of the line, and it has given me the greatest pleasure to produce the following information.

The research work for this project has taken many years, and has involved visiting the necessary record offices in Newcastle and Morpeth as well as London and Darlington. Considerable time has also been spent talking to the local people of Amble and the surrounding area, in addition to the railway specialists at Darlington.

Before this research came about, I had always had a fascination for railways – how they worked, the many different types of locomotives and rolling stock that graced the lines, and what was needed to operate the railway system. My interest grew from an early age having lived where the railway passed at the end of the street. It was always fun to run to the trackside, and climb the wooden fencing to poke my head over the top to watch what was happening – sooty locomotives taking clanking wagons back and forth from the sidings and moving them down to the harbour, and other locomotives and trains disappearing westwards under "Marks Bridge" into the distant unknown with their loads of empty coal wagons ready to be refilled.

My mother became seriously ill during 1962, so this was an opportune time for the family to take advantage of my growing interest. I was allowed to visit Alnmouth station regularly to train-spot on my own from the age of 12, the sandwiches packed, the flask of coffee made ready, a notebook in my haversack and off I would go. The short bus journey took me to Hipsburn for a five-minute walk up the bank to the station, and the family now knew where I was, conveniently out of the way, while they attended to my sick mother's needs! During that summer, and through my frequent visits to Alnmouth, I grew to love the steam locomotive and its working environment.

Although Amble, unlike Alnmouth, was on a branch line where trains operated less frequently, my interest in the development of the railway was intensified rather than deterred over the ensuing years. Amble owes its development to the growth of the local coal mining industry, while the railway provided the link from colliery to distribution point, culminating in the exportation of the coal from the harbour.

As with all railway branch lines, economics played a huge factor in the existence of Amble. Even after the closing of the unprofitable passenger service in 1930, Amble's branch line lasted until the end of coal mining in the area. The branch line survived all kinds of railway economic cutbacks over its life including the might of the British Railways Board and Dr. Beeching's "axe".

The history of Amble's township has been quite well documented, but this book attempts to explore the growth of the railways, including the small network of lines that were used to transport the coal from the collieries to the ships in the harbour. I hope that this book pays adequate tribute to the branch line's existence and to the people who worked on it.

Bartle Rippon
Perth, Western Australia, 2007

About the Author

Bartle Rippon was born in Amble in August 1950, living there until 1972 before leaving to attend the College of the Venerable Bede, Durham University. After gaining teaching qualifications, he taught in South Shields for the next 26 years before emigrating to Perth, Western Australia, with his wife and two of their three children, in 2001. (The eldest, being stubborn like her Dad, had other ideas!) Bartle is a very keen railway enthusiast, disco entertainer and football referee, who never misses an opportunity to visit his home town of Amble.

Chapter 1

Railway Days

At the end of our street ran the railway line down to the harbour. We would always know when trains had arrived as the crockery would rattle gently on the kitchen sideboard, and living in King Edward Street was almost as close as you could get to watch and feel the passing locomotives and their trains of coal wagons. The clanking noise of wagons being marshalled in the sidings became all too familiar, and the donk, donk, donk, donk, donk, donk, donk sound was to become one of my earliest memories.

I grew up with this noise and eventually, when my age allowed, I followed the sound to see exactly what was going on. Climbing the fence of old sleepers, and hanging on to the top for dear life, I could observe the movements going on with the locomotives and wagons. From this small beginning, I developed an interest in railways that was to remain with me for the rest of my life.

Other than collecting train numbers and having the traditional Tri-ang train set (which has since grown enormously) I eventually acquired a Kodak Brownie 127 camera in late 1964, and I could now go photographing the steam locomotives. However, teenage funds were very limited and there were times when opportunities were missed for a "shoot" – something I have regretted over the years! I took many opportunities to jump over the fence to catch sight of a steam locomotive, record its number and, where possible, photograph it! I was aware that this was really a trespassing offence, so I had to be careful which train to watch and which railway official was around.

I got to know Freddie Wake, the Station Master in the latter days of the railway at Amble. Exercising caution, I was able to wander about, keeping well out of the way of the train movements. The workers from the National Coal Board were not so generous, so being astute, I had my ways to keep out of sight – one skill I learned rather quickly!

On one occasion I was given permission to climb one of the signal gantries, and was carefully standing astride the rotting boards when an NCB locomotive with a solitary wagon came past. Not knowing whether I had been seen, I stood perfectly still, other than photographing the train, until the "danger" had passed. I descended the gantry and since

Dundee's last V2, 60836, makes a surprise visit to Amble with a load of coal on 27ᵗʰ May 1966. The locomotive had been on loan to Alnmouth shed while regular K1s were being serviced at Tweedmouth. Prior to this visit, the loco had been working the regular Alnmouth to Alnwick passenger service. The crew asked the author not to show this photograph to anyone, as the loco was really too large for the branch. Forty years after the event, perhaps it is now safe to do so! (Bartle Rippon)

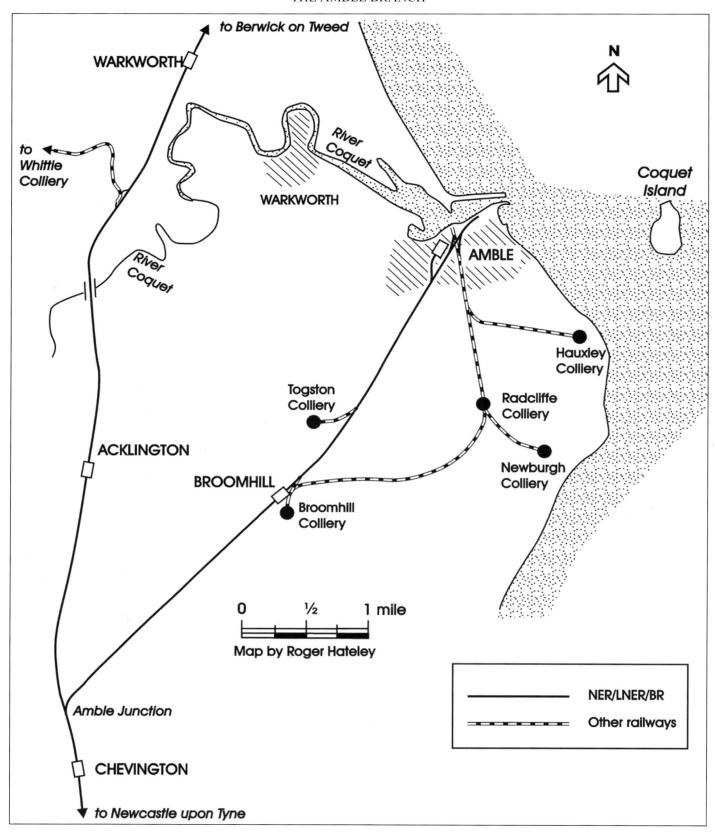

Amble and its environs, showing the main line, the branch line and the associated colliery network. (Map by Roger Hateley, published here with permission from "Railway Bylines" and Irwell Press)

then have admired the photo I managed to take *(see page 37)*. Amongst my early photography I took the opportunity to photograph Amble Station and goods yard, the harbour and many of the locomotives that came with their coal trains over the closing years of the railway.

Another interesting occurrence was when a large locomotive appeared at Amble bearing a load of coal. In my excitement I took its photograph, knowing I had something special. Then suddenly came shouts of perturbation from the locomotive's cab: "Bart, don't show anyone the photo!" I wondered for a while why, then I realised. This locomotive was really too big and too heavy to be on a branch the size of the Amble branch! However, this photo has become one of my many cherished possessions.

This was not all. Occasionally I would get a shout to jump aboard. Excitement abounded! I would run beside the moving locomotive, grab the handrail and then jump on to the step. Once on, I would climb into the cab and enjoy the heat, the workings and the views from the footplate. Only once was I not so successful in jumping aboard. Slipping off the wet step and hanging on to the handrail, I swung to the side, hit my leg and was left with rather a large bruise. It did not stop me enjoying my ride!

On another occasion, I had a footplate ride to Broomhill where I jumped off onto the old station platform. Sadly, I had no film left in my camera so a wonderful photographic opportunity passed me by. There were many other occasions where I was able to roam about on the railway line at Amble without being stopped and interrogated.

As the era of coal mining and exporting came to a close at Amble, I took as many photographs as possible and once even ventured along the railway line to Amble Junction. This was a beautiful hot summer's day out, and just being in the country was terrific, but this is where I noticed, even at this late stage in the branch line's life, what the line entailed.

THE HARBOUR, AMBLE G 8767

The Harbour, Amble from a postcard published around 1967. (Bartle Rippon Collection)

Overleaf: *A fine aerial view of Amble Harbour showing four of the five staiths. The tracks are quite full with coal wagons, while an NCB loco is taking a train of empties to Hauxley Colliery. There are four rows of houses at the bottom of the photograph in the middle, that end at the railway line at their eastern end. The author lived in the middle of the third row counting upwards. (Aerofilms Ltd)*

Chapter 2

Amble's Background

The beautiful coastal region of Northumberland lay mainly unspoilt for hundreds of years. Revolts amongst the early settlers did little to spoil the area; in fact they contributed to the changing landscape. But things were to change with another event that started early in the 17th century – the Industrial Revolution.

The small settlement of Amble was but a few homes perched on the south bank of the River Coquet, a coastal plain that exuded a "nothingness", but for a vast ocean of blue to the east and a gradual rising of the land towards the Simonside Hills in the distant west; no trees, no hills, just a soft undulating plain. The hamlet of Amble lay in the shadow of the mighty township of Warkworth, a village sporting a castle and church of Norman origins, steeped in history, the one-time home of the Hotspurs, later belonging to the Duke of Northumberland, and now in the caring hands of English Heritage.

Of Amble, McAndrews quotes in his book *Amble & District*:

"No proud, powerful baron by feats of arms in the battlefield or tourney has thrown a halo of romance round Amble. No marauding borderer has stained its annals with bloodshed, and the entire absence of any connection with troublesome times stamps its past history with the stamp of peace."

Amble's meagre history amounted to the unearthing of a stone coffin near the south pier in 1859, revealing Celtic human remains. Some 26 years later, excavations at the quarry revealed a graveyard of primitive settlers, presumably from the same period. Of Roman times, only a mere fragment of a stone altar was found at Gloster Hill. Also near here was once a Manor House that fell into disrepair, and by the late 1700s or early 1800s all that was left was a window, now preserved beside the Catholic church off High Street.

Amble, known earlier as Annabelle or Anna's Promontory, slowly began a livelihood where the townsfolk were largely engaged in farming and fishing. This is evident in the Government census of 1841, where the occupations show that a larger number of people were employed this way than in any other industry. Later Amble began to grow as coal was discovered in the surrounding area, and a demand for more workers to excavate the coal resulted in housing for the increasing population. Small cargoes of coal were now being exported regularly from the river mouth, staiths having first opened in 1835, so there was a need for some form of harbour to cope with the early demand for exported coal.

The mouth of the River Coquet became known officially as Warkworth Harbour in 1826, when an Act of Parliament was passed for the harbour's construction. It took that name as Amble had yet to develop into a significant township.

Noticing the number of collieries beginning to emerge and the waggonways being created, the aspiring York, Newcastle & Berwick Railway recognised the opportunity for exporting coal at Amble and applied to Parliament in 1845 to build a branch line from its main line railway to the port at Amble, the line opening on 5th September 1849.

Another view of the harbour showing the massive timber LNER staiths coming into the picture from the right. (Bartle Rippon)

NEWCASTLE AND BERWICK RAILWAY.

NOTICE.

OPENING OF THE LINE THROUGHOUT

FROM

NEWCASTLE TO BERWICK.

On and after **THURSDAY, 1st July,** the Line will be **OPEN THROUGHOUT FOR PASSENGER** and **GOODS TRAFFIC,** and the Trains will leave each Terminus at the following Hours :---

FROM NEWCASTLE.	FROM TWEEDMOUTH.
Morning - - - - - - 7.30, 10.30	Morning - - - - - - 6.30, 9.0, 12.0
Afternoon - - - 2.30, 6.40, 7.0, 11.30	Afternoon - - - - - - 2.30, 6.0, 7.45
SUNDAYS.	**SUNDAYS.**
Morning - - - - - - 10.30	Morning - - - - - - - - 12.0
Afternoon - - - - 2.30, 11.30	Afternoon - - - - 6.30, 7.45

In addition to the above, Trains will run between **NEWCASTLE** and **MORPETH** as under :---

LEAVE NEWCASTLE.	LEAVE MORPETH.
A.M. P.M.	A.M. P.M.
7.0, 6.0	SUNDAYS, 8.15, 5.45	8.0, 7.0	SUNDAYS, 9.15. 7.0

For further Particulars see Time Bills, which may be had at all the Stations.

BY ORDER,

JAMES ALLPORT,

MANAGER.

Newcastle, 26th June, 1847.

Amble would now see significant growth, becoming an urban council in the process, and having control of its own affairs – no longer would it be under the influence of Warkworth. Its industrial growth would eventually expand to incorporate a shipyard and brickworks, as well as engineering businesses.

Since the decline in mining, and the subsequent loss of trade to the harbour, Amble flourishes today as a holiday resort, a marina and a respectable small industrial town. The fishing industry was quite important within the town although it too has become a declining industry. Yet it is the production of coal that played such a significant part in the town's growth. Had it not been for the coal industry and the coming of the railway, it is doubtful whether Amble would have enjoyed the relative importance it has today.

The Collieries

Throughout nearly 150 years of coal mining in the area, there were several collieries, the first being Radcliffe, opened in 1836, which was followed by Broomhill in 1840. Togston Colliery followed in 1890 along with the Lady Newburgh colliery in 1892. From 1st November 1900, Broomhill Colliery took control of all mining in the immediate area and formed Broomhill Collieries Ltd.

Later, Togston would close completely owing to the collapse of its shaft, and Radcliffe succumbed to a geological fault, causing the end of mining by the 10th November 1896.

A new colliery at Hauxley was opened in 1926 and lasted until November 1966. Hauxley South Drift closed in 1951, while Newburgh colliery served as a ventilation shaft for Hauxley.

All these collieries finally came under the control of the National Coal Board as the result of Nationalisation in 1947. For all these collieries, a private railway network existed to operate and transport the goods to the harbour for export. As well as locomotives and rolling stock, Broomhill Colliery Ltd also owned the shipping fleet. This however, had become a separate company by 1936.

The Brickworks

Bricks were produced in Amble in quite large numbers. Radcliffe Colliery (which was taken over by the newly-formed Broomhill Collieries Ltd on 1st November 1900) had a by-product of clay, which was taken to Amble and used for making bricks. The colliery owned the brickworks at the harbour, and the majority of the output in the early days was used to build the expanding town. Some bricks were also sold around the country, being sent either by rail or ship. Oddly enough, the bricks were stamped with the name of Radcliffe!

The brickworks remained open until 1955, and had 8 kilns that in 1873 were producing 160,000 bricks a month; each kiln had the capacity to hold 6,500 bricks. A track led into the brickworks for the wagons to supply the clay.

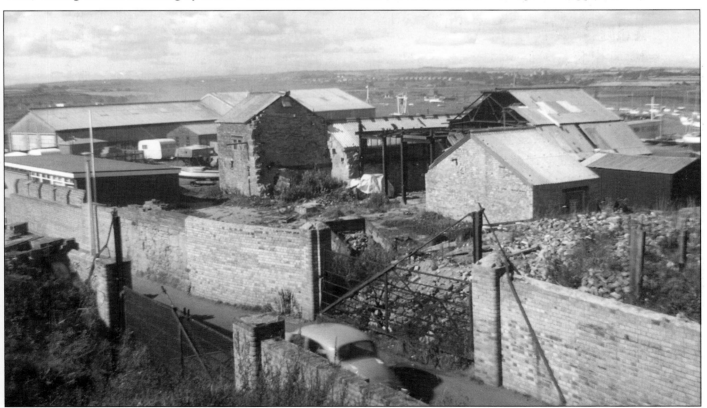

The remains of the brickworks in October 1969. The stone wall to the left of the gate is part of the original bridge that took the line over the harbour on a trestle. It is understood that some coal was also exported from the north pier. (Bartle Rippon)

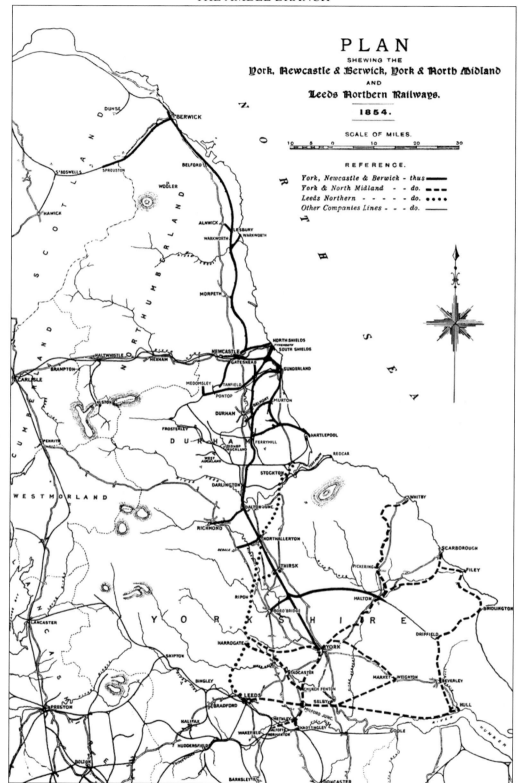

Dating from 1854 this map shows the York, Newcastle & Berwick Railway with a branch to Warkworth (Warkworth Harbour, Amble). The other notable feature is Lesbury, which was a very small station built to serve Alnwick before the Alnwick branch was built. This branch left the main line at Bilton Junction, which changed its name to Alnmouth station after merchants from that town requested a station. Alnmouth had its own harbour, exporting grain. Lesbury was short-lived but the building still remains today, just to the north of the "Eighteen Arches" viaduct that straddles the River Aln.

MAP OF THE NORTH EASTERN RAILWAY

AT DECEMBER 31st. 1922

North Eastern Railway Company's Lines including Joint Lines
Running Powers over other Companies' Lines
Other Companies' Lines

The North Eastern Railway at its zenith, just before the Grouping in 1923. The Alnwick branch is now extended through to Coldstream, and another coastal branch is shown – the independent North Sunderland Railway running from the main line at Chathill to Seahouses.

Two platelayers at work at Chevington station, showing the substantial house provided for the Station Master to the right.

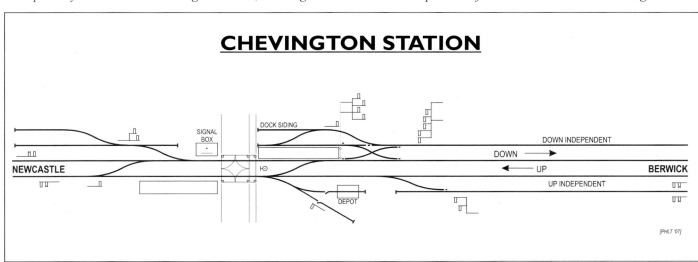

CHEVINGTON STATION

SIGNAL BOX

DOCK SIDING

DOWN INDEPENDENT

DOWN

NEWCASTLE

UP

BERWICK

DEPOT

UP INDEPENDENT

[PHLT '07]

Chapter 3

The Railway

The railway started its journey from the aptly-named Amble Junction on the East Coast railway line, about midway between Chevington and Acklington stations in Northumberland – a pleasant country location surrounded by Chevington and Eshott Woods, which were inaccessible by road! The line was almost five miles in length over the gently undulating plain sloping towards the coast, where no gradient was in excess of 1 in 177. In fact, it could be said that the scenery was pretty uninteresting, but careful observation would locate the ever-watchful Warkworth Castle that had stood in defence of this stretch of land for centuries.

The railway line was principally built as a mineral line for the export of coal from the local collieries, where Broomhill Colliery was its major customer and had running powers over the line to the harbour at Amble, formerly and quite fondly known as Warkworth Harbour.

Along the line's path there was a small level crossing near to the present-day prison. The road for this once gave access to RAF Acklington, a busy wartime fighter station, and after the War, it had a Spitfire to grace its gateway. The RAF station continued well into the late 1960s as a training station before changing hands to the Army, and finally becoming an open prison.

Further along the line was Broomhill Station, a single-line basic affair with a solitary platform building. From here the railway undulated its way towards Amble, passing the site of Togston (not that anyone would have noticed) then under a farm bridge before arriving in Amble. For the most part between Broomhill and Amble the railway was double line.

Once in Amble the scene was quite different. There were sidings, a goods shed, the station itself sitting proudly above Dilston Terrace, an NER signal box and an array of gantries adorning the area. The main tracks led to five staiths to offload wagons of coal to the waiting ships below. The station, which remained open for goods traffic after the passenger services ceased, included a large goods shed with a 3-ton crane outside, and several sidings for the storage of wagons.

Broomhill Colliery (sunk in 1773 to tap large reserves of good-quality steam coal) also had its own 1½-mile private railway line that extended from Broomhill towards Radcliffe and its former colliery (sunk in 1836), then straight to Amble arriving from the south, unlike the NER, which came in from the southwest. After the opening of Newburgh Colliery the colliery line was extended nearer to the coast to service it, and from Hauxley Colliery the rails came from the south to join those from Radcliffe, and then down to the harbour. This resulted in the crossing of railway lines at the top of Percy Street.

The passenger service was brought into operation in 1879, some 30 years after the opening of the branch line, and operated a shuttle service to and from Amble for connecting services to Newcastle at Chevington. It lasted until July 1930, when it was deemed that the service was no longer viable and was replaced by what was considered to be the more appropriate United bus service.

The Amble train waiting to leave Chevington station, c1900.   (Bartle Rippon Collection)

Top: *Chevington station down platform as it looked in 1955. The bay for the Amble branch was behind the station nameboard. (Bartle Rippon Collection)*
Bottom: *Chevington signal box, level crossing and down platform in 1955. (Bartle Rippon Collection)*

Coastward Bound from Chevington Station

Chevington station was on the main Newcastle to Edinburgh line almost a mile south of Amble Junction, making the passenger journey to and from Amble longer than the branch line itself, since there was no station at the junction. Situated between Widdrington and Acklington, there was nothing of great significance at Chevington other than a crossing point for local traffic. Initially there was only a cottage for the use of a gatekeeper for the railway crossing from 1847, but as road usage increased, better crossing gates and a signalbox were erected. The signalbox was of NER design, similar to those at both Warkworth and Alnmouth and other places along the railway; it contained 11 levers and a gate wheel.

From that time onwards the station grew, with the addition of a small coal depot and sidings, in the hope of attracting local agricultural business and also supplying their needs. Although Chevington station was on the main line from around 1870 (it first appeared in the public timetable in October of that year), it was not until Whit Monday, 2nd June 1879, some nine years later, that passenger services to Amble began.

Chevington station was not the traditional type with platforms directly opposite each other. Instead, the platforms were placed end to end on either side of the road with the gated crossing separating them, similar in style to Warkworth. The down platform, for passengers to the north and Scotland, lay to the north of the level crossing; it had a bay on its western side from where the passenger train to Amble would depart. Opposite the down platform, on the east side of the railway, was a two-siding goods yard with coal drops and a cattle dock.

The up platform, for passengers to Newcastle and further afield, lay to the south of the level crossing.

Due to the gradual increase of railway traffic heading in both directions and the Amble passenger service, the track was quadrupled northwards from Chevington Station to Amble Junction, although this did not occur until around 1900, nearly 50 years after the original opening of the main railway line and some 20 years after the commencement of the local passenger service.

The station buildings were small and not to any elaborate design or form, unlike Benjamin Green's designs at Acklington, Warkworth and other stations between Newcastle and Berwick. (Green had also been responsible for designing the impressive Theatre Royal in Newcastle.) With the exception of the Station Master's house and a couple of cottages owned by the railway company for use of railway employees, there were no other dwellings at Chevington other than those at Amble Junction itself.

A northward view of Chevington station taken in 1959, shortly after its closure to passenger traffic. (John Mallon)

Around the Chevington station area was an impressive array of signals, all of NER origin. The station was a busy place for its size and location, with stopping passenger trains going south and north, the branch line to Amble, and the many passenger expresses and goods trains that would be seen travelling through non-stop.

Passenger receipts grew as well as the goods receipts, the amounts differing depending on the direction travelled. In the 1928/9 period, the total value of traffic (passengers, goods and minerals) at Chevington heading towards Amble was just over £995, and in the opposite direction, just over £500.

Almost all the Amble branch passenger trains terminated at Chevington Station. The Amble trains originally arrived at the up main platform and departed from the down line, being stabled in the goods siding of the up line between services. However, after an accident on 25th October 1887, pressure was put on the NER to change the operation of the train arrivals and departures, and the Board of Trade appointed an independent observer, Major-General CS Hutchinson, to investigate the accident.

In his report, Hutchinson noted that five movements over the level crossing were necessary, in switching from the up to the down lines. He therefore recommended that the branch trains should have their own arrival and departure platform siding on the west side of the down platform –

hence the bay platform there.

There still remained the problem of congestion on the main line between Chevington and Amble Junction, so in 1913 the line was quadrupled between those places, the 1188yd loop line on the down side of the main line being upgraded for use as a passenger line. The points and signals at the south end of the loop were controlled from Chevington signalbox which, following alterations of 1913, had 37 working levers and 3 spare, while the points and signals at the north end of the loop were worked from Amble Junction signalbox, which had 61 levers and 1 spare.

Chevington eventually lost the regular passenger service to Amble from July 1930, but continued as a country station until it closed to all passenger services on 15th September 1958. Goods traffic was handled at the station for some years after that, but it closed to all traffic on the 10th August 1964.

The scene today is an automated barrier in place of gates for the level crossing, a building that is the remnant of the signal box and the former Station Master's house, which remains in good living order.

Chevington had its share of mishaps, including the aforementioned accident in October 1887 when a series of events caused severe damage to railway locomotives, rolling stock and permanent way. It was probably the worst experience the station was ever to encounter.

The Amble passenger train had been instructed by the

The accident at Chevington on 25th October 1887. (Ken Hoole Collection, Darlington Railway Centre and Museum)

Station Master to reverse on to the up main line to collect two cattle wagons. However, a southbound Tweedmouth to Newcastle express goods train failed to stop at danger signals just to the north of the station. It rammed into the local passenger train, pushing it into the goods train that had brought in the cattle wagons. As a result of the accident, three locomotives were badly damaged, two passenger carriages were written off and two goods wagons were completely destroyed. The damage was estimated at £1059, which did not include the cost of the damage to the permanent way.

Little information is given about the 13 passengers who were reportedly aboard the Amble passenger train, or the drivers and firemen of the three locomotives. JA Wells, in his book *Signals to Danger*, gives a more detailed timetabled account of the trains' movements that led to this accident. The events are recorded in Table 1, below.

There were other instances where railway practices appeared to give great concern to the travelling public. In 1888, the Local Board of Amble wrote to the NER requesting the resiting of the railway station at Chevington to Amble Junction itself. The Board complained about the workings of the Amble train at Chevington, as described in Hutchinson's accident report, and the expression of passengers that the up mail train passed almost simultaneously with the rear of the Amble train clearing the main line.

The NER's response was that practices were no different elsewhere on the company's railway, but that "many stations built many years ago are gradually being improved in point of accommodation and general public convenience".

No consideration appears to have been made regarding the inaccessibility of Amble Junction by road, although a cinder path led from Chevington station to the junction. Access could also be obtained over a farm track just to the south of Maiden's Hall Farm, but it was not suitable at certain seasons of the year! Jack Calvert mentions this farm track in his reminiscences of early life at Amble Junction, together with his regular journeys to and from school in Red Row during the very early 1940s.

Another incident involved the overnight Kings Cross to Edinburgh express, which became derailed just south of Chevington Crossing on 13th September 1913. It occurred at around 5.00am, as a signalman was going off duty and began to walk home. He heard the locomotive shut off steam, and looking to see why, saw sparks and stones flying through the air, so he jumped to the safety of the neighbouring field, and remained there until the dust had settled! JA Wells, in *Signals to Danger*, relates that the locomotive had been travelling at speed, and had not been notified of some speed restrictions that had been introduced as a result of permanent way work.

The last reported accident (*HMSO Railway Accident Report – 97042*) occurred just north of Amble Junction on 16th July 1967 when the southbound "North Briton" passenger train became derailed by a broken rail. Colonel WP Reed quoted in his report, "On a fine evening, 'The North Briton' from Edinburgh to Leeds, became derailed at a broken rail in the up line as it was travelling at speed of about 75mph." Colonel Reed praised the rescue by stating, "Finally I would like to draw attention to the expedition with which rescue and relief was organised at this somewhat remote site on a Saturday evening." Only 9 of the 160 passengers required hospital treatment, and none of them was seriously hurt.

Amble Junction

From Chevington Station, the railway progressed northwards and quickly reached Amble Junction. Here, on the eastern side of the main line, there were sidings and loops for the movement of coal wagons to Amble from the nearby collieries. There was also a coal washing plant, albeit hidden by trees, but it doesn't appear to have lasted long in service. CR Warn, in his book *Railways of the Northumberland Coalfield*, shows an undated map depicting coal screens, but by 1965, no evidence existed on OS map sheet 71. The only evidence I have located of something being there is through the personal recollections of Jack Calvert who, as a young

Table 1	
7.08pm	Up passenger train arrived from Amble. Passengers alighted and train was placed in down siding at 7.17pm.
7.30pm	A special down cattle and goods train arrived with 41 wagons plus brake van, including one wagon of cattle for Chevington and two for Amble at the front of the train.
7.36pm	Above train shunted through the south crossover on to the up line and drew forward to about the centre of the platform (this was to clear the down line for a local passenger train). Wagon of cattle pushed along by hand alongside cattle dock. Engine replaced the three wagons in siding, behind wagon of cattle. Engine moved on up line to clear the north crossover but stopped near the home signal, 160 yards ahead of its train.
7.42pm	Down passenger train from Newcastle to Alnwick arrived running eight minutes late.
7.44pm	Signalman accepted an up express goods from Amble Junction box. Put "on line" at 7.48 pm.
7.45pm	Alnwick train departed. Amble train pulled into down platform from siding and 13 passengers boarded. It was then drawn forward and reversed through the north crossover to attach the two cattle wagons from the goods train still standing on the up line and take them to Amble. It was for this reason that goods engine was kept clear, but this was a most unusual manoeuvre.
7.52pm	Express goods, Tweedmouth to Newcastle Forth failed to stop at signals at danger. Travelling at over 20mph it violently rammed the stationary engine, bulldozed it into the passenger train, which was then moving towards the crossover back to the down line, and slithered it back into the goods train.

Amble Junction looking north, viewed from the signal gantry in around 1910. The Amble branch is seen curving away to the right and six railwaymen's cottages sit in the "V" of the junction. (J Mallon, Darlington Railway Centre and Museum)

boy, lived at the "Junction Cottages" during the very early 1940s. He stated that "small spoil heaps of shale were evident amongst the wood".

Amble Junction was an imposing scene with its 62-lever signalbox straddling the main railway line high above the running tracks. Along with this was a myriad of signals and gantries constantly in use as trains clattered by in each direction on a regular basis. Nestled in the fork of the mainline and the branch to Amble stood several railway cottages where a small community of railway employees and their families existed.

From the signalbox, the signalman had an excellent view of the tracks both north and south, and from the top of the steps leading to the cabin, a view to the coast. It had no amenities, so if the signalman needed to answer a call of nature, he would visit the bushes and trees on the western side of the railway!

The signalman was a lifeline for the nearby railway cottage dwellers. Should an emergency occur, they were allowed to call the signalman who, in turn, made it his duty to summon help. The signalbox ceased to function during 1933, just a few years after the branch passenger service to Amble

was withdrawn in 1930, and control of the junction was taken over by Chevington signalbox. All goods operations for the branch were now run on the up slow or goods line, a way of working that continued officially until December 1942, when the up and down loops were recommissioned, and the points at Amble Junction were electrically operated from an improved signalbox at Chevington Station.

The impressive signal cabin was to meet an untimely fate when it was partly damaged by fire on 20th August 1937, never to be restored to working order. By that time, however, Chevington signal box had taken control of all the signalling in the area and left the Amble Junction box redundant. It was still in its original state until then, but was permanently locked and unused up to 1942. In October of that year, it was dismantled owing to the redundant steelwork being required, presumably for the war effort. The brick supports remained in place until around the late 1950s, or early 1960s.

Immediately to the north of the junction signal box, as the railway curved eastwards towards Amble, it passed the railway cottages and sidings (usually full with empty and loaded coal wagons), and onto the single track section that would take the trains to the coast.

Amble Junction today is no more, and all traces of its existence have disappeared. Only a small road now passes alongside the railway, as it makes its way over the formation of the branch line towards Acklington Prison.

AMBLE JUNCTION

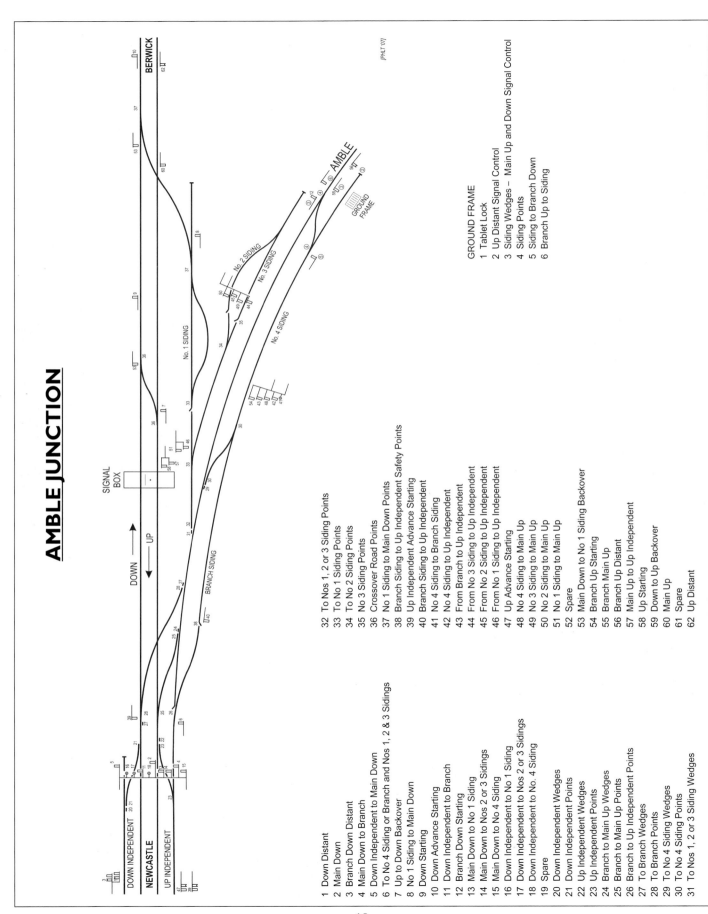

1 Down Distant
2 Main Down
3 Branch Down Distant
4 Main Down to Branch
5 Down Independent to Main Down
6 To No 4 Siding or Branch and Nos 1, 2 & 3 Sidings
7 Up to Down Backover
8 No 1 Siding to Main Down
9 Down Starting
10 Down Advance Starting
11 Down Independent to Branch
12 Branch Down Starting
13 Main Down to No 1 Siding
14 Main Down to Nos 2 or 3 Sidings
15 Main Down to No 4 Siding
16 Down Independent to No 1 Siding
17 Down Independent to Nos 2 or 3 Sidings
18 Down Independent to No. 4 Siding
19 Spare
20 Down Independent Wedges
21 Down Independent Points
22 Up Independent Wedges
23 Up Independent Points
24 Branch to Main Up Wedges
25 Branch to Main Up Points
26 Branch to Up Independent Points
27 To Branch Wedges
28 To Branch Points
29 To No 4 Siding Wedges
30 To No 4 Siding Points
31 To Nos 1, 2 or 3 Siding Wedges

32 To Nos 1, 2 or 3 Siding Points
33 To No 1 Siding Points
34 To No 2 Siding Points
35 No 3 Siding Points
36 Crossover Road Points
37 No 1 Siding to Main Down Points
38 Branch Siding to Up Independent Safety Points
39 Up Independent Advance Starting
40 Branch Siding to Up Independent
41 No 4 Siding to Branch Siding
42 No 4 Siding to Up Independent
43 From Branch to Up Independent
44 From No 3 Siding to Up Independent
45 From No 2 Siding to Up Independent
46 From No 1 Siding to Up Independent
47 Up Advance Starting
48 No 4 Siding to Main Up
49 No 3 Siding to Main Up
50 No 2 Siding to Main Up
51 No 1 Siding to Main Up
52 Spare
53 Main Down to No 1 Siding Backover
54 Branch Up Starting
55 Branch Main Up
56 Branch Up Distant
57 Main Up to Up Independent
58 Up Starting
59 Down to Up Backover
60 Main Up
61 Spare
62 Up Distant

GROUND FRAME

1 Tablet Lock
2 Up Distant Signal Control
3 Siding Wedges – Main Up and Down Signal Control
4 Siding Points
5 Siding to Branch Down
6 Branch Up to Siding

Amble Junction signalbox c1910. (Ken Hoole Collection, Darlington Railway Centre and Museum)

Amble Junction signalbox piers still standing long after its demolition. (John Mallon)

Above: *The water tower and crane at the start of the branch from the main line to Amble. (Bartle Rippon)*
Left: *The Township crossing lady, Mrs. Harmerson, c1922.*

Township Crossing

Leaving the hustle and bustle of the busy railway junction, the railway ran out into the peaceful Northumberland countryside. Coming into view next would be Township Crossing – a simple affair of gates where a small country road (believed to be called Green Lane) crossed the railway track. There was also a ground frame hut (or small signalbox) housing the equipment to operate the gates. The limited available information does not give a detailed picture of what was actually there.

The crossing gates were operated for many years by an elderly person who, upon hearing a bell, would promptly close the gates to the road traffic, and allow the unimpeded journey of the train. It is interesting to wonder how much local road traffic there would actually have been!

Although Government census details reveal that William Bowey (aged 69) was gatekeeper in 1891 and William Rochester (aged 68) was gate keeper in 1901, notes from a copied diagram of the crossing gates show that one keeper was Mrs Harmerson, who held the post from 1921 until the end of passenger trains in July 1930. It appears that the duties of the crossing were not onerous and therefore suited an elderly person to operate them.

The same diagram states that the public by-road was used very little prior to World War II, and had since closed due to the building of the aerodrome. The gates stood padlocked across the railway because of considerable RAF road traffic, and were opened only by the train crew. They had become responsible for the operation of the gates after the cessation of passenger services in July 1930. The change of procedure was noted in the following way:

AMBLE BRANCH:
WORKING TOWNSHIP LEVEL CROSSING GATES, BETWEEN CHEVINGTON AND BROOMHILL

The level crossing gates must stand normally across the railway, and remain padlocked in this position until required to be open for rail traffic.

When it is necessary to open the gates for rail traffic, they will be opened by the fireman of the train using the branch; when the train has been brought to a stand at the crossing, the fireman must open the gates, secure them across the roadway, and after satisfying himself that it is safe to do so, lower the signal for the driver to proceed, and rejoin his engine.

When once the gates have been placed across the roadway for the passage of a train, they must remain in that position until the train has passed clear of the crossing.

When the train is clear of the crossing, the Guard must close the gates across the railway, padlock them in this position, and place the signal to danger, afterwards rejoining the train.

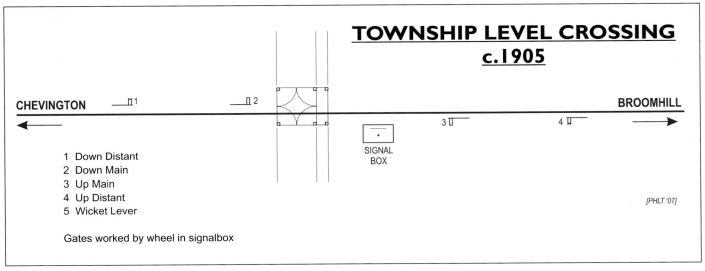

TOWNSHIP LEVEL CROSSING
c.1905

CHEVINGTON

BROOMHILL

1 Down Distant
2 Down Main
3 Up Main
4 Up Distant
5 Wicket Lever

SIGNAL BOX

Gates worked by wheel in signalbox

[PHLT '07]

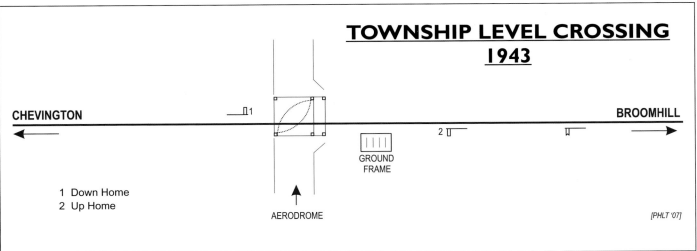

TOWNSHIP LEVEL CROSSING
1943

CHEVINGTON

BROOMHILL

GROUND FRAME

1 Down Home
2 Up Home

AERODROME

[PHLT '07]

Top: *A busy morning platform full of passengers awaiting the arrival of the train from Amble. Amongst the passengers is a group of army personnel, the date being c1910. The ever-popular OXO gravy advert shows that is was just as popular towards the start of the 20th century as it is today. (Bartle Rippon Collection)*
Bottom: *A quiet Broomhill station around 1915. (KL Taylor)*

Broomhill station with "Cadets of the Temperance" waiting to leave on their annual day out during 1907. This might take them to many places, from Whitley Bay to Berwick and even Wooler. (Bartle Rippon Collection)

Broomhill Station

Broomhill was the only intermediate station on the branch, and was situated almost halfway between Amble Junction and Amble, 2m 33ch west of Amble and 2m east of the junction. It had a single platform of 99½ yards, with a building similar in design to that at Chevington. It was built in 1878, and opened to passenger traffic with the branch on 2nd June 1879. The cost of building amounted to £262 19s 6d.

During 1911, Broomhill flourished, with tickets sales totalling 27,746 – amounting to over 500 tickets per week. There were five trains each way on weekdays and eight on Saturdays. There was also a late-night Amble to Broomhill train that allowed revellers the chance to return home after a night out in Amble, probably frequenting the local public houses as well as the Central Hall that stood beside the Metal Bridge in Dilston Terrace, next to the station.

Excursions were popular, and it was not uncommon for family parties and organisations to venture on a day out. This can be seen by the photograph of a party of Temperance families waiting patiently for their train to begin their day away (above). Excursions would take them to places such as Whitley Bay, Berwick and even as far away as Wooler.

Along with the station itself, Broomhill boasted a small goods yard, a signalbox, the Station Master's house and several cottages for its employees. The goods yard had two sidings together with a warehouse and a 30cwt crane, as shown on the Engineers' Department map of Broomhill dated 1943. The sidings themselves were 155 and 173 yards in length with a capacity for wagons of 118 and 135 yards respectively. Broomhill had a total of 590 yards of railway track for storing goods traffic and other rolling stock.

Following the closure of the station to passenger traffic on 7th July 1930, the building remained for some time while goods traffic continued to be handled. The goods depot eventually closed on 4th May 1964, but the goods yard remained in use as a storage area. This was evident, particularly during the mid-1960s, when the sidings were used to store empty coal wagons during the "Pitman's Annual Holidays" for two weeks during July.

By this time, the main station buildings and signalbox had long disappeared, but the warehouse remained, and was used by a private owner. Only the platform itself remained intact, although a small platelayers' building had been erected; all signalling and point operation was now handled by a 6-lever ground frame that allowed for all train movements, including those of the NCB colliery.

After the closure of the signalbox, a ground frame was introduced about 1943, with the following Chevington to Amble instruction issued *(overleaf)*:

BROOMHILL COLLIERY BRANCH:

This Branch is worked in accordance with the Regulations for working Single Lines by One Engine in Steam, and all Drivers must be in possession of the Train Staff before leaving Chevington.

A Ground Frame is provided at Broomhill Colliery.

Three stop boards lettered STOP UNTIL AUTHORISED TO PROCEED BY PERSON-IN-CHARGE and fitted with white lamps are provided at Broomhill Colliery as follows:

Down Direction   One 30 yards on Chevington side of ground frame.
Up Direction   One 105 yards on Amble side of ground frame.
Sidings   One between Mineral siding and the New Outcrop sidings.

After the cessation of the passenger service in 1930, and the consequent closure of the station, the buildings were removed and the fences taken away. This can be confirmed some thirty years later from the view of the last passenger train to visit the branch in September 1963. A group of onlookers is admiring the event as the train heads towards Amble, and the overbridge can be clearly seen to the west of Broomhill's platform. It is interesting to note the aforementioned small shed standing on the platform, erected for the use of the permanent way staff as a shelter during their duties along the branch.

The Broomhill area would continue to be a busy place, even though the colliery closed in early 1964. The administration for the colliery works continued at Broomhill, and maintained its locomotive shed right up until the end of all railway workings.

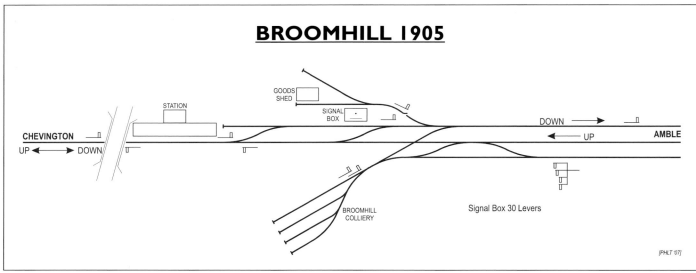

BROOMHILL 1905

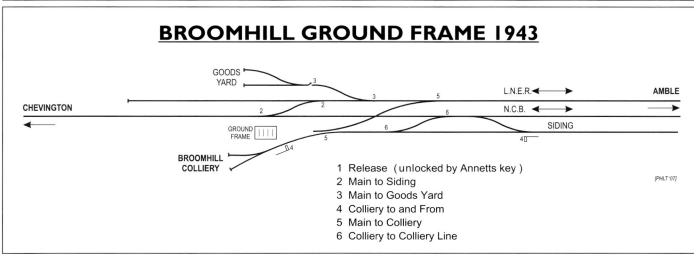

BROOMHILL GROUND FRAME 1943

1 Release (unlocked by Annetts key)
2 Main to Siding
3 Main to Goods Yard
4 Colliery to and From
5 Main to Colliery
6 Colliery to Colliery Line

A view of onlookers at Broomhill Station as the last passenger excursion visits Amble on 29th September 1963.
(DK Jones Collection)

Broomhill Colliery Railway

Broomhill Colliery came into existence around 1840, and was originally owned by Earl Grey. It changed hands several times, and during the 1850s, the owners were Burdon & Co, Messrs Sowerby & Andrews subsequently taking charge around 1890. On 1st November 1900, the colliery took control of all the other collieries in the area, changing its name from the Broomhill Coal Co Ltd to Broomhill Collieries Ltd.

The coal shipments from Broomhill to Amble were originally worked by gravity, and the empty wagons were worked back to the colliery by horses. At some time during 1854, records show that Broomhill Colliery had at least one locomotive, although what it was it is not recorded.

Broomhill Colliery joined the branch line to the east of the station platform. The colliery railway merged from the south, and a double line resulted for the remaining journey to Amble.

Initially, the colliery shared the running of the railway with the NER from this point all the way to Amble. As the increase in coal production continued, more colliery trains were needed to transport their loads to the harbour, and other trainloads of coal for export were coming in via the branch line from other collieries such as Shilbottle.

The single railway line was becoming increasingly congested, and the resulting delays to coal movements meant that ship-loading and the subsequent seaward journeys were affected. To overcome this congestion, the Broomhill Coal Co promoted a Parliamentary Bill in the late 1880s for the construction of the Broomhill & Amble Railway. This would have been an independent line between the colliery and Amble. By the early 1890s the proposed new line had still not materialised and the congestion had become more problematical in 1892 with the opening of Togston Colliery.

This line was to run from Broomhill Colliery, through Radcliffe, and enter Amble from the south. The Broomhill Co continued to encounter considerable problems trying to obtain the necessary powers for its new line so an agreement was reached between the Broomhill Coal Company and the NER to double the track between Broomhill and Amble. This agreement of 1893 superseded the Broomhill & Amble Railway Bill.

The NER would now double the existing line, be responsible for its maintenance, and provide 180 yards of extra siding accommodation at Amble for Broomhill Colliery use, as well as for other traffic.

The new double track was inspected by Major-General Hutchinson for the Board of Trade on 28th September 1894. He reported that the double-track section was 2 miles 33 chains in length, and incorporated three new overbridges and three new underbridges. It was noted that the station at

Broomhill had not been altered, the double-track section stopping short of the actual station.

The alterations required revised signalling arrangements, so Broomhill signalbox now comprised 24 working levers and 6 spare.

The Broomhill Colliery Co was permitted to use the up line between the passing of the last NER train at night and 6.00am the following morning. The working was by means of a brass train staff that was handed by the Broomhill signalman to the driver of the colliery loco, which could then work throughout the night as required.

Although the Broomhill Colliery Co had running powers, the responsibility for the maintenance of the line fell wholly to the NER. For the colliery company's part of the running power arrangement, Broomhill Colliery would provide its own locomotives, carriages and wagons, and pay the NER for the use of the railway between Broomhill and Amble, for the shipment of:

- Round coal at 9d per chaldron (3.39d per ton).
- Small coal at 8d per chaldron (3.10d per ton).
- Carriages for conveying workmen, £250 per annum as long as colliery workmen are conveyed.

Broomhill Colliery, while using railway and works, agreed to abide by the rules and regulations of the NER. This agreement was signed by Richard Jack, for and on behalf of Broomhill Coal Co Ltd and J Shillito, for and on behalf of the NER, at York.

For Broomhill Colliery workers, a passenger service was provided by the company from Amble to the collieries as part of the agreement. The carriages used for the workmen's trains were old NER 6-wheelers, which remained in operation until about 1927, when they were withdrawn because their deteriorating condition made them unsuitable for transporting the men. The service lasted for about 33 years, but where this train began and terminated in Amble is open to conjecture! It is unlikely that the coaches ever used the platforms at either Broomhill or Amble stations.

Several years after the implementation of the double line, permission was given to Broomhill Collieries Ltd to open another railway link through Radcliffe and into Amble from the south. This was, in fact, the original proposal by the Broomhill Coal Co Ltd and finally came into operation around 1900/01.

This railway line went from Broomhill eastwards, turning towards Radcliffe and then directly to Amble. A railway connection was made to link the Lady Newburgh Colliery to Radcliffe. This colliery was sunk in 1892 after Radcliffe Colliery had become unworkable due to a huge geological fault that prevented further coalmining. Another colliery was to eventually supersede the Lady Newburgh Colliery, this one being at Hauxley in 1926. This railway would eventually be extended for the coal traffic from Hauxley Colliery to Amble after its opening.

Togston Colliery Junction

After leaving Broomhill Station, the railway gently undulated through a cutting towards the coast, and Togston Colliery sidings came into view.

At the beginning of April 1892, Togston Colliery Junction was added to the branch line for the transportation of coal from the colliery. It began as a single siding linked to the branch and operated by a 6-lever ground frame. As the colliery grew in production, greater congestion of the use of the single line became more apparent. The railway line to Amble having been doubled, more sidings were added to this small junction. A signalbox was added also, containing 12 levers of which 3 were spare.

One of the NER carriages used by Broomhill Colliery near Amble signalbox awaiting departure to Broomhill – both men and boys are sitting and clinging to the carriage. The chap hanging on to the end is Thomas Beaty, the father of the family who have kindly loaned this photograph. It would have been taken any day of the week except a Monday as Thomas always found getting to work a little difficult after an enjoyable weekend! Judging by the condition of the carriage, it must be around 1925, shortly before it was withdrawn. In the same train can be seen a private owner wagon of Broomhill Colliery.
(Courtesy Mrs Ella Lillico)

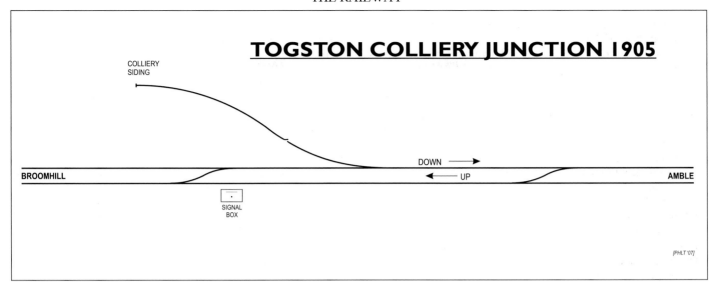

TOGSTON COLLIERY JUNCTION 1905

COLLIERY
SIDING

DOWN →

BROOMHILL

← UP

AMBLE

SIGNAL
BOX

[PHLT '07]

The junction remained this way until the unfortunate early closure of the colliery due to the surrounding clay causing the partial collapse of the pit shaft. This was the final attempt to mine coal in the Togston area. There had been several attempts since 1826, and coal from the Togston area was being shipped from Amble ten years before the Warkworth Harbour Act was obtained in 1836. (Further details of this activity can be found in *Amble & District* by TL McAndrews.)

Following the closure of the short-lived Togston Colliery, the sidings became redundant and were finally closed. So too was the signalbox, which closed at 10.00am on Monday 17th May 1909. "All signals and connections will then be dispensed with", was the mandate from the NER. The junction remained for a short time afterwards before all evidence of its existence was finally removed. No trace of the colliery or its sidings can now be found.

*An early locomotive being brought in by ship to be assembled, possibly for Radcliffe Colliery before the branch line to Amble was opened, or alternatively for use in the construction of the North Pier.
(Colin Wood)*

Amble Station

From Togston, the railway trundled past Hope Farm entering Amble through an under-bridge known as Marks Bridge. On entering Amble, the railway became three lines before branching out to sidings and the goods yard. This is how the railway layout finally evolved.

The railway to Amble had existed since the construction of the York, Newcastle & Berwick Railway in 1847, and as the line was basically for mineral use, there was no station although the layout was quite modest. In addition to coal from the Togston area, which as already noted had been exported from the harbour as early as 1826, coal was also being exported by Earl Grey's colliery at Radcliffe and Broomhill where horse-drawn coal trucks were regularly handled between the colliery and the harbour.

Prior to the YN&BR's construction to Amble, a steam locomotive was reputedly in use. This might have been shipped in by sea, before being assembled and used on the construction of the harbour. The photograph on the previous page certainly suggests this, and the locomotive could well have been used in the construction of the north pier, traversing the River Coquet by means of a trestle bridge.

In 1876, nearly thirty years after the opening of the railway, the NER put forward a proposal for a station at Amble, which would also include a warehouse and goods siding. At this time the approach to the planned station was from an overbridge immediately to the west of the station site.

On 27th April 1878, a building plan was presented to Alnwick Rural District Council for the construction of a two-storey station building and platform. The station building would incorporate the station offices at platform level, while underneath would be a residence for the Station Master and his family. Building took place in 1878, and was completed in time for passenger traffic to begin from 2nd June 1879.

The platform was approximately 300 yards in length, and the building included a ticket office, waiting rooms and storerooms; there was also an additional wooden building for extra storage.

At the east end of the station there was a water tower for servicing the locomotives, similar in design to the one at Alnwick Station. (It was removed shortly after passenger working ceased, leaving only the concrete base and drain as evidence of its existence.)

Access to the station was from Dilston Terrace, up the newly-formed Station Road, and the station building was built on the north side of the railway tracks leading to the staiths. The later Station Master's house and other cottages for the railway employees were built along this short approach to the station. As the railway grew in size, other railway cottages were added in the locality, mainly in Percy Street on the south side of the railway.

In 1892, the layout was quite compact, and a single line

The train waiting at Amble station prepares for another journey to Chevington. The loco is NER 2-4-2T No 1160. Note the Broomhill Colliery private owner wagons to the right. (Ken Hoole Collection, Darlington Railway Centre and Museum)

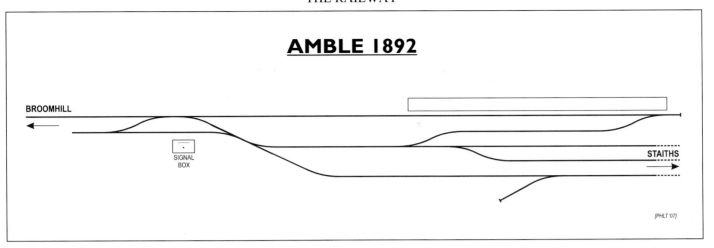

AMBLE 1892

BROOMHILL

SIGNAL
BOX

STAITHS

[PHLT '07]

led to the station platform, while sidings were provided for the coal wagons prior to being unloaded at the staiths; the Metal Bridge carried only two railway lines.

A small signalbox stood on the south side of the tracks and contained some 14 levers.

The original layout of the railway at Amble was eventually to be abandoned for an improved version, resiting the goods warehouse and rebuilding the Metal Bridge over Dilston Terrace to take three tracks. The original signalbox therefore had to be dismantled, and it was replaced by a larger one near the 4¾ milepost, some 500 yards west of the

station. This new box had 45 levers, and this number was eventually increased to 50. By 1909, the layout at Amble had stabilised, and was to remain in that form until its closure.

There was now an attractive array of lattice-post signal gantries around the area, mostly with lower-quadrant semaphore arms. Until their final demise in January 1965, they remained *in situ* after the closure of the signalbox, although without their signal arms. A photograph depicts the event in the *Northumberland Gazette* of 5th February 1965, but sadly no records have been kept.

The goods yard had a warehouse, a dock and a 3-ton

The Amble train waiting at the station. The water tower can clearly be seen between the train and the Broomhill Colliery coal wagons. (Ken Hoole Collection, Darlington Railway Centre and Museum)

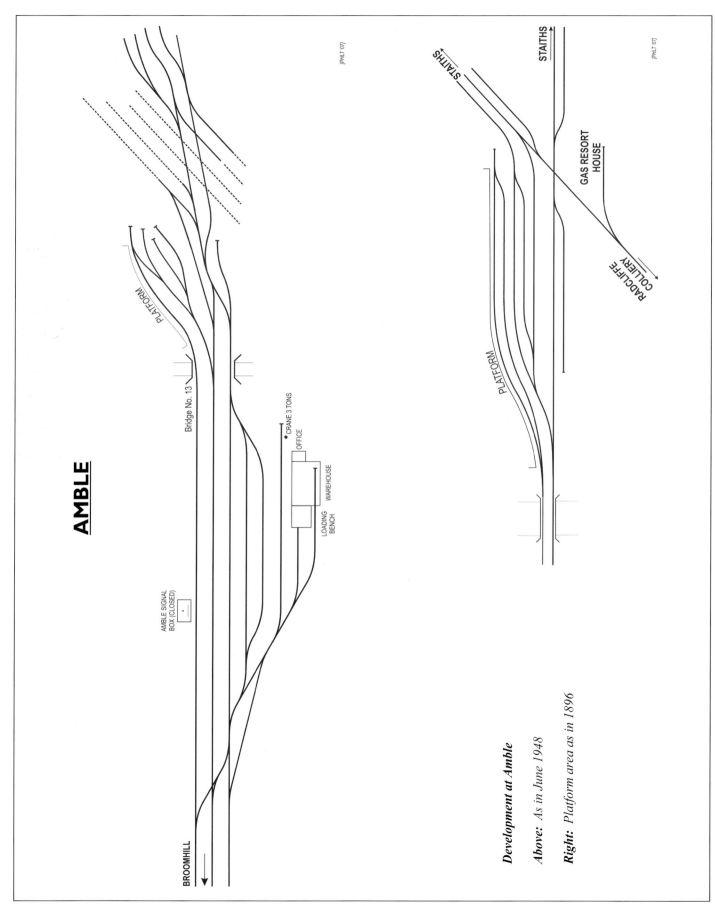

AMBLE

BROOMHILL

AMBLE SIGNAL BOX (CLOSED)

Bridge No. 13

PLATFORM

CRANE 3 TONS
OFFICE
WAREHOUSE
LOADING BENCH

[PHLT '07]

STAITHS

STAITHS

GAS RESORT HOUSE

RADCLIFFE COLLIERY

PLATFORM

[PHLT '07]

Development at Amble

Above: *As in June 1948*

Right: *Platform area as in 1896*

NER class F (later LNER D22) 4-4-0 No 18 with driver George Dodds in around 1922. (J Mallon)

crane; also in the goods yard was the Consolidated Petroleum Co, an office and a weigh-bridge. On the opposite side of the railway line, almost facing the station, were two more NER buildings for railway employees, and attached to one set of buildings were stables for the horses used to deliver the goods from rail to door in the surrounding neighbourhood. There was even a piggery run by one of the NER workmen! This was noted on one of the early plans showing land ownership kept in the Northumberland Record Offices.

By 1894, the line was doubled into Amble due to the increased congestion of rail traffic. Once in Amble, goods branched off to the sorting sidings, one of 246 yards and two of 203 yards in length. There was also a shorter siding of 176 yards. From the sorting sidings, wagons would be sent to the coal staiths for unloading, while any traffic for the goods yard would be stationed on the 176-yard siding.

A storage siding of 281 yards in length was adjacent to the running lines into Amble from the western overbridge known as Marks Bridge. This was the extra accommodation that had been provided by the NER in their agreement of 1894.

The 3-ton crane was near the eastern end of the goods shed siding, and a smaller siding of 52 yards led to the loading bay, while a 98-yard siding went into the goods shed itself. The coal hoppers were usually left in the sorting sidings, and the duties of marshalling them to the staiths and replacing the empties fell to the Broomhill Colliery engines.

The Branch Line Terminus

The actual end of the branch line was at the staiths where the coal, for which the line was built, was exported. There were five staiths in total, four owned by the collieries and one by the NER (later the LNER). They were designed by Thomas Meikle & Sons, as was the harbour, and were built during the early or mid-1800s.

The colliery-owned staiths would take one wagon at a time to unload its cargo to the waiting ship below. This work was done by a set of men called "teemers", while the "trimmers" were inside the ship's hold to even out (or "trim") the load by distributing it into the corners – not an easy or particularly safe job. Once the individual wagons had been unloaded, they were led away down a gradient to be taken away by the locomotive.

The NER staith could handle up to four wagons at any one time, but the cargo was discharged in a similar way.

Part of number two staith had coal drops beneath it where coal merchants could benefit from the task to supply the Amble residents with fuel for their homes and businesses. This was situated behind the Warkworth Harbour Commissioners' stores and existed until the end of coal shipments.

The rest of this chapter features photographs of Amble station environs and the line to the staithes.

Top: *A rake of coal hoppers adorning the platform at the station. It is 24th August 1962, and the nameboard is still in place, although the name is not discernable. (Ken Hoole Collection, Darlington Railway Centre and Museum)*
Bottom: *Amble station building on 29th September 1963. The station buildings are contained within the upper storey, while the ground floor would have originally been for the Station Master. (RM Casserley)*

Two views of Amble station looking forlorn, empty and deserted in October 1969. (Bartle Rippon)

Top: *Amble station falling to bits! It is October 1969, the top rails of the fence have fallen off, and part of the platform has collapsed. Soon there will be nothing left. (Bartle Rippon)*
Bottom: *Looking west, the buildings visible left to right are two NER employees' cottages, the goods shed, the girders of the bridge over Dilston Terrace and a wooden storage building on the platform itself. (Bartle Rippon)*

The west end of the goods shed (top) looking very overgrown. No longer do the rails exist to allow wagons full of cargo to enter and leave the building. The view past the shed (bottom) shows the loading dock and the 3-ton crane. (Bartle Rippon)

Top left: *A solitary gas lamp still standing like an ever-faithful sentinel in October 1969.*
(Bartle Rippon)

Top right: *The 3-lever ground frame. Left to right, lever 1: home signal, lever 2: colliery signal, lever 3: points.*
(Bartle Rippon)

Far left: *A North Eastern Railway slotted signal post that has been adapted. This signal post remained until the closure of the railway line.*
(John Hinson Collection)

Near left: *The NER slotted signal post standing on the NER staiths; the slot can be clearly seen.*
(John Hinson Collection)

The drain and base of the water crane at the east end of the station platform. (Bartle Rippon)

Looking towards the staiths in the summer of 1964. The coal hoppers on the left are using the approach road to the station, and an NCB tank locomotive is taking a solitary coal hopper towards the harbour. (Bartle Rippon)

Looking east towards the station and harbour – empty coal hoppers adorn the line into the station. The single slip allows access to other parts of the station yard. The small building to the right is the platelayers hut, and beside this, but not visible, is the ground frame. (Bartle Rippon)

Amble looking towards the staiths on 29th September 1970. From the left, trains would arrive having passed the station, the line continuing out of picture to the right taking the wagons to the NER staith. From the bottom-right are the lines from Hauxley Colliery and Broomhill, leading straight ahead to numbers 4 and 5 staiths. (KL Taylor)

The approach to No 5 staith on 29th September 1963. A rake of wagons is already waiting to be unloaded to the ship below. The return line for the empty wagons can be seen to the right, and the remains of the track bed to the left would probably have taken the train to the north pier via the wooden trestle bridge during the construction of the harbour. (HC Casserley)

Looking towards the NER staith from the level rail crossing (top) and looking back towards the crossing and the station in the opposite direction in September 1970. (KL Taylor)

The NER staith showing the winding gear for the chute and the covered coal drops where, after discharging their loads to the waiting ship below, up to four wagons at a time would roll on to the siding to be dispersed. (Top: KL Taylor, bottom: Bartle Rippon)

The massive structure of the NER staith seen from below. (Top: KL Taylor, bottom: Bartle Rippon)

The NCB staiths in around 1970, showing (left) the "head" of No 5 staith. The wagons would be drawn up this point, one at a time, to dispatch their cargo to the waiting ship below, after which the wagons would be despatched along the return road to the right. It was not uncommon for a wagon to overshoot the end, and on one occasion it was thankfully saved by the chute in its "up" position! The "teemers" hut is on the right.
(Top: KL Taylor, left: Bartle Rippon)

From the NER staith looking westwards (or upstream) is a wonderful aspect in around 1970 of the NCB staiths, the old mooring jetty from the shipyard days, a flotilla of moored pleasure craft and the distant Warkworth Castle. (Bartle Rippon)

Just to the west of No 5 staith, stands Harrison's boat yard around 1970. Much of the area lies derelict but is soon to be altered as Amble begins the construction of its marina on the distant flat land that was once occupied by the shipyard. (Bartle Rippon)

A view looking over the top of the Warkworth Harbour Commissioners Stores towards the remnants of Nos 2 and 3 staiths around 1970. It was in this area that coal drops were made for the local coal merchants to supply the needs of the townsfolk. (Bartle Rippon)

From the end of the NER staith looking eastwards towards the harbour mouth are two mobile conveyors. These were used for a short time when grain was exported, and also minerals, as can be seen from the stocks heaped in the area. The south pier was still in reasonable repair at this time, around 1970. (Bartle Rippon)

Chapter 4

Train Services

Passenger Traffic

Passenger trains ran from Amble to Amble Junction and then along the NER main line to Chevington station, where passengers could change for trains to Newcastle, Berwick and all stations north and south.

As seen from the working timetable of 1930 *(see Appendix A)*, there were six down passenger trains and seven up passenger trains each weekday. The first train of the day departed from Amble at 7.42am and would return with the 9.26am from Chevington. Saturdays had seven workings with the addition of a late night departure at 10.40pm from Amble to Broomhill and return. The 12.23pm Saturday-only working from Amble continued through to Morpeth to become the 1.15pm return to Amble.

Carriage stock was stabled at Amble Station overnight, while the engine returned to Alnmouth, and returned the following morning. The locomotive assigned to run this service was NER class A 2-4-2T No 55. It worked chimney first to Amble and tender first to Chevington, spending the entire day operating the service. From time to time, as

repairs and servicing necessitated, a replacement locomotive would be seen performing the passenger duties.

There is no clear picture about the types of locomotive used on the Amble Branch, but occasionally the branch line would be graced with larger NER Class M 4-4-0 locomotive types.

The locomotive and crew began the day leaving Alnmouth at 7.00am. They would then travel to Amble to begin the day's first duty at 7.30am. The last working of the day would see the locomotive leaving Amble for Alnmouth at 8.15pm on weekdays and 10.25pm on Saturdays. For the crew, the day was not quite as long as it would seem, since two sets of men were assigned to the duties. The first set began their day at 5.40am, finishing at 3.40pm, while the next set of men took over at 12.50pm and completed their shift at 11.05pm – still a long day at work compared to the modern working day. This information is given in the North Eastern Railway's *Passenger Engine Working Timetable* of 1908 *(overleaf)*. There was no Sunday service.

A memorandum outlining the viability of the passenger service was discussed by the LNER's Traffic Committee on

The Amble branch train was regularly hauled by NER class A (LNER class F8) 2-4-2T No 55. While there are no photographs of it in action on the branch, it is seen here at Berwick shed. (A Murray Collection)

			a.m.		
Alnmouth	...	...	...	7 0	L E
Amble	...	...	7 30	8 0	
Chevington	...	...	8 15	9 30	
Amble...	...	...	9 45	10 26	
Chevington	...	...	10 41	10 57	
Amble	...	...	11 12	11 23	
Chevington	...	...	11 38	11 53	
Amble	...	...	12 8	2 13	
Chevington	...	...	2 28 *	2 50	
Amble	...	...	3 5	5 13	
Chevington	...	...	5 28	5 55	
Amble	...	...	6 10	6 45	
Chevington	...	...	7 0	7 53	
Amble	...	...	8 8	8 15	L E **S**
Alnmouth	...	...	8 40		

	1st set.	2nd set. **S**	2nd Set. **S O**
	a.m.	p.m.	p.m.
Men sign on ...	5-40	12 50	12 50
	p.m.		
Men sign off ...	3-40	10 50	11 55
Hours on duty	10 0	10 0	11 5

Additional on Saturdays only by engine of No. 4 turn.

				p.m.
Amble	...	...	...	12 18
Morpeth	...	...	12 55	1 5
Amble	...	...	1 41	...
Amble	...	...	...	3 15
Chevington	...	...	3 30	3 45
Amble	...	...	4 0	...
Amble...	...	...	...	8 25
Broomhill	...	...	8 32	8 40 Ety
Amble	...	...	8 49	9 20
Chevington	...	...	9 35	10 0
Amble	...	...	10 15	10 25 L E
Alnmouth	...	...	10 55 p.m.	

the 29th May 1930:

"There has been such a considerable falling off in the passenger traffic on the branch that the service is being worked at a loss and the traffic is so small that it does not justify the maintenance of a service by a passenger steam coach (a steam railmotor).

"During the year ended the 30th June 1929 the estimated passenger and parcel revenue local to the branch amounted to £787. The contributory passenger receipts from the branch amounted to £3,489. It is assumed that the withdrawal of the passenger train service will result in the loss of one-third of the contributory receipts, viz £1,163. Without giving credit for the Railway Company's share in any of the passenger traffic, which will be diverted to omnibus companies, it may be assumed that the loss of revenue will amount to £1,950 (£787 plus £1,163).

"The expenditure incurred on the branch during the year ending 30th June 1929 has been apportioned between passenger and goods train working, and it is estimated that if the passenger service is withdrawn the annual saving will be at the rate of approximately £3,399 per annum, without taking credit for any saving there may be in maintenance of the permanent way. Deducting from this sum the essential loss of revenue amounting to £1,950, it will be seen that the net estimated saving resulting from discontinuation of the passenger service is at the rate of £1,449 per annum.

"It is considered that the service operated in the district by the United Automobile Services Ltd (*an LNER associated bus company*) will adequately meet requirements, and that no serious inconvenience will result from the withdrawal of passenger trains, which is anticipated will effect a nett saving estimated at £1,449 per annum. The estimated loss from parcels traffic is £1,046 but it is considered that this loss may be averted to a large extent by the employment of a 2-ton motor vehicle, to be stationed at Amble, to deal with the

A northbound express hurtles through Chevington station in the late-1950s or early-1960s, hauled by streamlined A4 Pacific No 60004 "William Whitelaw". Although the shed plate is unclear, it is known that this engine was shedded in the late 1950s at Haymarket (64B), and it is likely that this was the locomotive's home at the time this picture was taken. (JW Armstrong Trust)

A view of 43057 (top) at the head of the RCTS/SLS North Eastern Tour train at Amble station, taken from Station Road. 29th September, 1963 would be the last time Amble would ever be graced with a passenger train, and its patrons made the most of the opportunity to survey the station at Amble before it was gone forever. (Top: HC Casserley, bottom: DK Jones Collection)

whole of the parcels work including collection and delivery."

The committee therefore recommended that the branch passenger services should be withdrawn as from the 7th July of that year, an additional saving being "one radial tank engine type F8 and a train set consisting of 260 seats". The withdrawal was effected on the recommended date, but in the absence of Sunday services the last train ran on Saturday 5th July 1930. The station was officially closed to regular passenger traffic on the 7th July 1930.

The last passenger train to enter Amble Station was an excursion on Sunday 29th September 1963 organised jointly by the Railway Correspondence and Travel Society and the Stephenson Locomotive Society. This brought about a high level of excitement, not only for the passengers, but also to the residents close to the line, who could enjoy watching a passenger train! The train was headed by a Darlington-based locomotive, Ivatt class 2 2-6-0 No 43057.

Looking west towards Marks Bridge from the footplate of Alnmouth's K1 62012. (Bartle Rippon)

Goods Traffic

Coal had been the predominant traffic on the line ever since it opened in 1847, and as coal production increased, both the local population and local industry grew, hence the need for other goods to be brought in and out of Amble.

Coal production from the several collieries in the neighbourhood was high. During 1911, coal exports at the harbour were as high as 618,361 tons, and this was probably the busiest period the harbour had ever experienced. Trains of coal wagons would be brought into the sidings ready to be taken to the staiths for export by ship. The wagons would then be taken away and refilled.

The NER worked many goods trains in and out of Amble and this led to a creation of regular goods train workings.

Local farmers benefited in a small way when a cattle train was worked "as required" on Monday mornings only, provided there was sufficient livestock to fill a minimum of two cattle vans; it took cattle to the Newcastle markets. There was a "south and north goods pick-up" that visited Amble when required, conveying the goods traffic in both directions.

The northbound train usually originated from Heaton, Newcastle, and travelled all stations to Alnmouth. For the reverse working, the southbound goods train originated from Alnmouth and travelled all stations to Heaton, Newcastle.

By 1960, nearly all the general goods traffic was taken to Alnwick before being sorted and distributed around the Amble area by road vehicle. The author enjoyed many a trip around the Amble area in a British Railways Scammell driven by Frank Clegg, a driver at Alnwick. Some goods traffic also came from Morpeth.

In later years, the goods shed, although looking in good repair, became dormant. However, goods traffic did arrive, specifically for businesses in the town. An example of this was three vans full of empty milk crates and bottles from Darlington that were unloaded for Charlton's Dairy by the author and other employees of RH Charlton in the mid-1960s.

Also, a single Anglo-Scottish car-carrier van was noted by the author in Amble goods yard during December 1963 – delivering cars! During the late 1950s, it had been known for a circus to arrive at the station. Some of the larger animals, such as the elephants, were walked to where they were going to perform. Other than this spasmodic traffic, the goods shed stayed permanently closed. The goods shed buildings remained *in situ* until the early 1970s, after all the track and station buildings had been removed.

War Time

There appears to be no information as to the effect that World War I had on this branch line, but a little information is available regarding what happened during World War II. According to the author's father, who was stationed at the Army Coastal Defence barracks, some special passenger workings were made from Amble during the early years of that war. He apparently used them to travel to Morpeth and sometimes Newcastle, but records have proved extremely difficult to find regarding this.

A very poor quality photograph *(below)* shows Amble schoolchildren rehearsing the role of the evacuees in readiness for such an event, so that the local authorities could prepare themselves to handle the situation.

Freddie Wake, the last Station Master of Amble, who still lives in the old Station Master's house, has stated that evacuees were brought to Amble during 1940. Amongst

them were two teachers and two children who resided with Mr Arthur Bird, the Station Master at the time.

Amble was not entirely free from attack, as enemy aircraft were always in search of RAF Acklington, only three miles along the railway. On one occasion, Tuesday 3rd June 1941, an enemy aeroplane attacked the pit screens at Hauxley, the Amble Coastguard Station, the Amble Coastal Defence Camp and the foot of Queen Street known as Redman's Corner. It also fired on High Street, the brickworks, the signalbox and a train standing in Amble Station. Known casualties included an injured RAF corporal of the Marine Section, who was taken to RAF Acklington, and the guard of the train standing in the station, who was taken to Alnwick Infirmary, having been struck on the head by a bullet.

Other small incidents occurred around the area and railway line according to *North-East Diaries 1939–1940* by Roy Ripley and Brian Pears. The night of 17th/18th August 1941 saw ten high-explosive bombs fall in fields near Hope House Farm, either side of the railway. This could have been a misguided attempt at bombing RAF Acklington. Another night of action was 24th/25th June 1941, when three high-explosive bombs fell on the private colliery line between Broomhill and Radcliffe, rendering the line out of action. However, nothing was to compare with the bomb that fell on Radcliffe during the night of 15th/16th February 1942; it killed 3 people and injured 21.

Ivatt 4MT 43101 is placing its train into the sidings before collecting empties and moving away on 2nd August 1966.
(Bartle Rippon)

On 19th August 1966, Ivatt 4MT 43071 has just set its train into the sidings and is waiting for the fireman to tend to the coal in the tender before moving away. The platelayers' hut can be seen above the right buffer. (Bartle Rippon)

Chapter 5

Locomotives

Branch Locomotives

Details of the locomotives that worked the branch line in the early days seem to have gone unrecorded, but it is known that by the early 1920s, NER F class (later LNER D22) 4-4-0 No 18 was the regular branch passenger engine *(see page 31)*. It was the general practice to work tender first to Amble and smoke-box first back to Chevington, however this wasn't always the case! The LNER report of 1930 refers to a Worsdell F8 2-4-2T (NER class A) being the regular passenger engine at that time, and occasionally, a class M 4-4-0 would be seen on passenger duty.

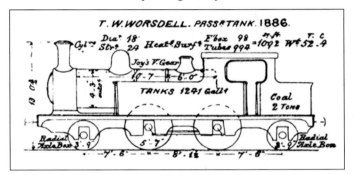

As for the goods motive power, in LNER days class Q engines, and later class R locomotives (LNER D20) could also be seen at Amble. During British Railways days, Gresley class J39 0-6-0 locomotives were regular visitors along with class J27 (NER class P3) 0-6-0 locos. From 1963, Thompson class B1 4-6-0 engines frequented the area along with the examples of the ubiquitous Thompson class K1 2-6-0. As the end of steam on British Railways was drawing to a close, many varied types of 2-6-0 locomotives could be seen as they finished their working lives.

Quite often, the class of locomotive was determined by what Alnmouth engine shed had available at that time. This was most evident when perhaps the most interesting locomotive to be seen at Amble arrived during 1966. It was Gresley class V2 2-6-2 60836, which was temporarily allocated at Alnmouth shed during May of that year.

After the demise of the steam locomotive, English Electric Type 3 diesels were regular visitors. It was not unusual to see these engines jumping the rails on the single-slip crossover, and this meant a call for the Heaton breakdown train to come and do a swift rerailing job.

Colliery Locomotives

The first locomotive recorded at Radcliffe was an 0-6-0ST built by Robert Stephenson & Co, Newcastle. This may have been used in the construction of Warkworth Harbour by the Commissioners, and is later said to have worked there. It might also have been the locomotive used in transporting the stone from the quarry to the harbour. This came about when

Warkworth Harbour Commissioners bought control of Radcliffe Colliery for a short period of time.

A Board of Trade report from around 1873 relates to the explosion of a locomotive boiler with a cylindrical firebox built in about 1843. Could this have been the locomotive that worked here before the existence of Amble's branch line?

A 2-4-0 NER locomotive built by Charles Tayleur, Newton-le-Willows (later to become the Vulcan Foundry) in 1839 was due to be purchased by the owners of Radcliffe Colliery but there are no records showing that the purchase ever took place.

Radcliffe Colliery purchased a further four locomotives built by Andrew Barclay Sons & Co Ltd of Kilmarnock, Ayrshire. They were 0-4-0ST outside cylinder locomotives. No 147, built in 1873, went new to the colliery but had been dispensed with by 1900, probably going for scrap. No 663 was given the name *Radcliffe No 2*, while No 742 was named *Lyne*. No 849 eventually had the distinction of being named *Radcliffe No 3*.

These locomotives were all absorbed into Broomhill Collieries Ltd on 1st November 1900, and all were transferred to Broomhill Colliery where repairs and maintenance could be carried out; Radcliffe's engine shed closed as a result.

At Broomhill, there was a small fleet of 0-4-0 and 0-6-0 types. Four were built by Andrew Barclay, and another four by Hawthorn Leslie & Co of Newcastle, between 1872 and 1882. Many of the tank locomotives carried names of the area, including were *Broomhill*, *Agnes*, *Wansbeck*, *Acklington*, *Coquet*, *Radcliffe*, *Aln* and *Blyth*.

It was also quite common for collieries to buy locomotives from around the country, and Broomhill was no exception as noted by the presence of three Great Western Railway locomotives. No 2199, originally with the Neath & Brecon Railway, was bought in 1932, and worked at Broomhill until its withdrawal in 1955. No 805 from the Rhonndda & Swansea Railway was bought in 1934, lasting until withdrawal in 1954. No 312 purchased from the Llanelly & Mynydd Mawr Railway in 1932 lasted until 1961. All three locomotives were bought through R Frazer & Sons Ltd, Hebburn, County Durham.

There was also a Southern locomotive, originally London Brighton & South Coast Railway No 607, that was bought through the same suppliers in August 1936.

Other locomotives came and went, including a class J94 that was hired from NER, but was never returned. There is also mention of an ex-War Department locomotive, No 75316, which arrived in July 1947.

All these remaining locomotives became part of NCB North Northumberland Area 9 from the 1st January 1947, and subsequently Area 3 from 1st January 1964.

A summary of the colliery locomotives under NCB ownership is given in Appendix B.

Ex-GWR 0-6-0T No 312 was shedded at Broomhill Colliery from 1935 until it was withdrawn in 1961. (Bartle Rippon Collection)

NCB No 28 is shunting another load of coal towards the staiths in around 1963. The train is composed of ex-Broomhill colliery wooden wagons of various sizes and appears to be standing over the Metal Bridge. Between the colliery wagons and the coal hoppers can be just seen one of the two remaining NER signals. The 0-6-0T locomotive with outside cylinders was built by Hudswell Clarke, Leeds in 1949, and came new to Broomhill, working the Amble Branch for almost its entire life with short spells at Ashington (presumably after heavy repairs, etc). (Bartle Rippon Collection)

K1 62023 reverses to attach the guards van to a rake of empty hopper wagons at Amble on 2ⁿᵈ July 1965. The 52D shed plate is that of Tweedmouth, the parent shed of Alnmouth, which provided the locos for the Amble branch. Formerly a Blaydon engine (52C), it came to Alnmouth in November 1962 until the closure of the shed, after which it was transferred to Sunderland (52G). (Bartle Rippon)

The sun shines kindly on K1 62030 as it shunts its train in the sidings. The distant row of houses is on St Cuthbert's Avenue, and this view indicates how flat the area was. The shadow of the home starter signal can be seen cast by the summer sun of 1966. (Bartle Rippon)

Alnmouth's K1 62006 sets its train back into the sidings ready to be taken to the harbour on 23rd February 1965. The platelayers' hut was a useful place to seek refuge on a cold wet day! (Bartle Rippon)

Alnmouth's class K1 2-6-0 62021 is shunting coal hoppers in Amble yard, while NCB 0-6-0T No 28 waits to take them down to the staiths on 13th May 1965. (Bartle Rippon)

Class Q6 63402 languishes, preparing to collect yet another rake of hopper wagons on 15th May 1964. This is an unusual visit for this type of locomotive, as they more often spent their time trundling around the more undulating Tyneside. It was a North Blyth (52F) engine, having arrived from Blaydon Shed (52C). (Bartle Rippon)

North Blyth's J27 65862 is busy shunting its train into one of the storage sidings on a summer's evening, 20th August 1964. (Bartle Rippon)

The evening summer sun in August 1964 glints along the boiler of J27 65882 as it awaits final instructions from Station Master, Freddie Wake, before setting off on its journey homewards. (Bartle Rippon)

Class 2MT 77002, a Tweedmouth engine, is slowly moving its train into the sidings in the summer sun before moving to collect its train for the return journey on 25th August 1965. (Bartle Rippon)

A wet day in 1965 sees K1 62006 leaving the sidings for its return journey westwards, having collected its train of empty wagons. There appears to be a leak around the cylinders judging by the amount of steam escaping. (Bartle Rippon)

On 19th February 1965, K1 62050 has collected its train on the station approach line and prepares to leave. (Bartle Rippon)

Chapter 6

And Finally...

Having flourished as a mineral line for all its life, and flirted with a short-lived passenger service, it was inevitable that closure would come as the coal reserves began to diminish in the area and the collieries became unviable. 1968 was the last year that coal was exported, as the steam locomotive had given way to diesel, and oil was now the required fuel; North Sea gas played its part too. Amble was now only visited by diesel locomotives.

From 1970, the railway infrastructure was dismantled, and all that was left was a mere "bed" that had already implanted a scar on the landscape. During the dismantling of the railway, the miners took strike action against the Government, which meant that our household, as well as many others, was short of coal for heating. To overcome this problem, I took the opportunity of "borrowing" a railway sleeper! Sneaking along the "back lane" to what was left of the railway, I pounced upon one and, lifting one end, suddenly realised how heavy these things are. Not to be discouraged, I dragged it single-handedly, and with great difficulty, half the length of King Edward Street and into the back yard of our house. It amazed me not only how big these sleepers were, but also what wonderful heat they generated once they had been cut into useable pieces!

It seemed to take a much shorter time for the railway to disappear than it did to construct, and in many ways, it resembled a model railway, with considerable time spent planning and building but being easy and quick to dismantle. With the disappearance of the railway and coal industry, there was an immediate effect on the economy of the local town. Jobs were lost and new opportunities were sought for the working population of Amble.

The excitement of a visiting train would no longer be experienced, and that last passenger train to visit the station in September 1963 had brought the station alive with the buzz of people. The passengers on the excursion spent their short time inspecting the railway by walking around the station and the surrounding area. After this fleeting visit, it was a sad occasion when the train left on its journey southwards. No more would Amble be graced with a passenger train. No more would the people see or enjoy the presence of a train like this.

Gone too were the days of the weekday washing being coated with soot from the passing locomotives, the rattling of crockery on the sideboard that announced the movement of trains, the dust and dirt from the coal operations, and the excitement at the end of the street!

My only regret throughout these days was in not taking enough photographs of the railway and the shipping, but this was due to the small budget of a youngster – not even the paper round provided adequate funding!

To fulfil the expectations of this book I have searched for, requested and borrowed all kinds of information to compliment my own records. I have been given some wonderful items and information, and I am extremely grateful for this. I still feel there is more to obtain about the people who worked on the railway between Amble and

The changing scene before closure. English Electric type 3 Co-Co No D6827 brings coal into Amble on 16th August 1966. (Bartle Rippon)

Amble Junction, and would like to think that if enough information was forthcoming more could be written. I should therefore be delighted to hear from anyone who may have information or photographs to contribute.

With this recollection of photographs, plans, diagrams and some memories it is hoped that what was once a busy mineral line, forgotten to the railway enthusiast, will now be remembered for many, many years to come.

Two views at Amble after the railway gangs had moved in and lifted the track in about 1970. On the left is a view westward looking towards Marks Bridge – a vehicle can just about be made out in the distance. On the right is a view taken on the same day looking eastwards towards the harbour. Only one small portion of track remains, but it will not be there for long. The building to the right is the goods shed. (Bartle Rippon)

Still remaining today on the east side of the level crossing at Chevington is the Station Master's house. The building was looking in a very good, attractive condition when photographed on 2nd June 2006. The main line is now electrified and the level crossing gates have been replaced with automatic half-barriers. (Kestrel Collection)

Contrasting views of Chevington. Looking south in 1959 (top), the home signal near the box has been cut down to leave only the sidings-to-main bracket on the post, and a new upper quadrant home signal has been erected near the end of the platform. The box was enlarged in 1923 when the Junction box closed and a larger frame was installed; the new stonework is just discernable to the left. Compare this with what remained of Chevington signalbox on 2nd June 2006. The top has gone leaving only the Northumberland sandstone base that now houses the relays for the crossing barriers and signals for the immediate area. The 1923 extension gives the locking-room windows an off-centre appearance. (J Mallon and Kestrel Collections)

Having been loaded with coal at the LNER staiths, the MV Bishorst waits to leave Amble on 25th August 1965. The ship, part of the Carsten Rehder fleet, had been built in 1953, and was a typical small Dutch Coaster. She now sails as the Loznati, and flies the Croatian flag. (Bartle Rippon)

SS Thrift – almost the last, if not <u>the</u> last, steam ship to enter the harbour, pictured here on 30th July 1966. She was built in 1931 and sold for scrap in September 1968. (Bartle Rippon)

Public and Working Timetables

Chevington and Amble.

DOWN. — WEEK DAYS.

	Light Engn a.m.	Goods E a.m.	Pass. a m	Pass. a m	Goods F p m	Pass. p m	Pass. p m	Pass. p m	Emp. Train D p m
Alnmouth .. Dep	7 0	..	9 40	11 42	..	2 50	5 57	7 47	..
Chevington .. ,,	..	..	..	..	..	..	..	..	..
Amble Junction ,,	7 20	7 35	..	..	1 10	..	..	..	..
Broomhill .. ,,	..	..	9 49	11 51	..	2 59	6 6	7 56	8 30
Amble .. Arr	..	8 10	9 58	12 0	1 40	3 8	6 15	8 5	8 39

UP. — WEEK DAYS.

	Pass. a m	Pass. a m	Goods p m	Pass. p m	Pass. p m	Pass. p m	Light Engn C p m	Pass. D p m	Light Engn D p m
Amble .. Dep	8 25	10 25	12 20	2 5	5 10	7 5	8 15	8 15	8 45
Broomhill .. Arr	8 34	10 34	..	2 14	5 19	7 14	..	8 24	..
Amble Junction .. ,,	..	..	12 50	..	..	..	..	..	..
Chevington .. ,,	8 43	10 43	..	2 23	5 28	7 23	..	..	..
Alnmouth .. ,,	..	..	..	..	..	..	8 50	..	9 20

C—Saturdays excepted.
D—Saturdays only.
E—Stops at Broomhill when required to detach wagons.
F—Works wagons of Mineral traffic for the North from Broomhill to Amble Branch Junction.

The working timetable for 1898.

Chevington and Amble.

Cattle Traffic.—Cattle traffic for Amble will be forwarded from Chevington by passenger train, provided the vehicles are fitted with Westinghouse pipe and screw couplings. The passenger trains will, when required, work one or two wagons of goods on the branch.

CHEVINGTON and AMBLE.—North Eastern.

Down. Week Days.

Miles		mrn	mrn	aft	aft	aft	aft	aft	aft
690	Central Station, Newcastle ..... dep	8 10	10 27	12 12	1 30	2 27	4 50	6 30	8 35
	Chevington ..... dep	9 30	11 53	1 26	2 50	3 45	5 43	7 53	10 0
3¼	Broomhill	9 38	12 1	1 34	2 58	3 53	5 51	8 1	10 8
5¼	Amble ..... arr	9 45	12 8	1 41	3 4	4 0	5 58	8 10 15

Up. Week Days.

Miles		mrn	mrn	aft	aft	aft	aft	aft	aft	aft
2¼	Amble ..... dep	8 0	10 26	12 18	2 13	3 15	5 13	6 45	8 30	10 45
5¼	Broomhill	8 7	10 33	12 25	2 20	3 22	5 20	6 52	8 37	10 52
	Chevington 690, 691 ..... arr	8 15	10 41	12 33	2 28	3 30	5 28	7 0	8 45	
31¼	691 Newcastle (Cen.) ... arr	9 12	12 12	1 34	4 25	6 30	6 37	8 27	10 5	

The public timetables for 1910 (above) and September 1929 (below).

CHEVINGTON AND AMBLE

WEEKDAYS

	Page	a.m.	a.m.	a.m.	a.m.	p.m.	p.m.	p.m.	p.m.
York ..... dep	40-43	5 12	—	10 5	10 5	—	2e3	3 40	6 15
Darlington ..... ,,		6 7	8 35	11 11	11 11	12 32	2c59	4 37	7 17
Newcastle ..... ,,	52-54	8 15	10 22	12 23	1 30	2 25	5 16	5 58	8 57

		a.m.	a.m.	SO a.m.	SX a.m.	p.m.	p.m.	SO p.m.	p.m.
CHEVINGTON ..... dep	52-59	9 26	11 31	1 36	2 15	3 33	6 2	7 12	10 5
Broomhill ..... ,,		9 34	11 39	1 44	2 23	3 41	6 10	7 20	10 13
AMBLE ..... arr		9 41	11 46	1 51	2 30	3 48	6 17	7 27	10 20

WEEKDAYS

	Page	a.m.	a.m.	SO p.m.	SX p.m.	p.m.	p.m.	p.m.	SO p.m.	SO p.m.
AMBLE ..... dep		7 42	10 40	12 23	1 30	2 37	5 18	6 27	8 45	10 40
Broomhill ..... ,,		7 49	10 47	12 30	1 37	2 44	5 25	6 34	8 52	10 47
CHEVINGTON ..... arr	52-59	7 57	10 55	12 38	1 45	2 52	5 33	6 42	9 0	

	Page	a.m.	p.m.	p.m.	p.m.	p.m.	p.m.	p.m.	p.m.
Newcastle ..... arr	56-58	9 7	12 15	2 10	3 42	3 51	6 39	7 40	10 h3
Darlington ..... ,,	47-50	10 29	1 f45	3 38	—	4 57	8 1	8 56	12 g14
York ..... ,,		11 35	2 38	4 43	—	5 50	9 8	9 41	1 g10

c Passengers can leave at 4.9 p.m. by Pullman Car Express to Newcastle (*see inset facing page 108*). e Passengers can leave at 2.42 p.m. and travel by Pullman Car Express from Darlington to Newcastle (*see inset facing page 108*). f Until 14th October arrives at 1.52 p.m. g Sunday mornings. Commences 22nd June 1930. h Commences 21st June 1930. SO Saturdays only. SX Saturdays excepted.

CHEVINGTON and AMBLE—Weekdays.

DOWN.

		1	5	5	6	7	11	13	15	16	17	18	19
		Light Engine.	B Goods.		PASSENGER.	PASSENGER.	PASSENGER.	PASSENGER.	PASSENGER.	PASSENGER.	PASSENGER.	PASSENGER.	Empty Train.
							SO	SX				SO	SO
M.C.		G a.m.	B a.m.	a.m.	a.m.	a.m.	F p.m.	p.m.	p.m.	p.m.	p.m.	p.m.	p.m.
.....	Chevington ... dep.	—	—	—	9 35	11 33	1 36	2 2	3 45	6 10	7 20	10 17	—
0 68	Amble Junction ⊕ „	7 11	8 43	9 5	..	..	..	..	..				—
3 28	Broomhill ...... ⊕ „	....	9 15	9 50	9 43	11 41	1 44	2 10	3 53	6 18	7 28	10 25	10 54
5 62	Amble .. .. arr.	7 20	9 58	—	9 50	11 48	1 51	2 17	4 6	6 25	7 35	10 32	11 1

B—Heaton Junction dep. 7.10 a.m., p. 11.
F—Morpeth dep. 1.15 p.m., p. 12.
G—Alnmouth dep. 6.55 a.m., p. 16.

UP.

		1	2	5	5	6	8	9	11	12	13	14	16	17
		PASSENGER.	PASSENGER.	D Goods.		PASSENGER.	PASSENGER.	PASSENGER.	PASSENGER.	PASSENGER.	Light Engine.	PASSENGER.	PASSENGER.	Light Engine.
				arr.	dep. SO	SX					SX	SO	SO	SO
M.C.		N a.m.	a.m.	a.m.	B a.m.	E p.m.	p.m.	p.m.	p.m.	p.m.	G p.m.	p.m.	p.m.	V p.m.
.....	Amble ... ... dep.	7 40	10 40	—	10 48	12 23	1 35	2 33	5 18	6 33	7 45	8 45	10 40	11 8
2 34	Broomhill .. ⊕ „	7 47	10 47	10 56	11 20	12 30	1 42	2 40	5 25	6 40	..	8 52	10 47	..
4 74	Amble Junction ⊕ arr.	....	....	11 30	11 50	....	....		....		7 55	....	....	11 18
5 62	Chevington .. „	7 55	10 55	11 30	—	12 38	1 50	2 48	5 33	6 48	—	9 0	—	—

B—Heaton Junction arr. 2.7 p.m., p. 18.
E—Morpeth arr. 1.0 p.m., p. 18.
G—Alnmouth arr. 8.15 p.m., p. 14.
N—Morpeth arr. 8.19 a.m., p. 16.
V—Alnmouth arr. 11.35 p.m., p. 14.

The working timetable commencing 9th July 1923.

CHEVINGTON and AMBLE—Weekdays

		1	2	3	4	5
	DOWN		D Goods			
M.C.			A a.m.			
.....	Chevington ... dep.		*			
3 28	Broomhill ...... ⊕ „		*			
5 62	Amble .. .. arr.		DD			

		1	2	3	4	5
	UP			D Goods		
M.C.				V a.m.		
.....	Amble ... ... dep.			U		
2 34	Broomhill .. ⊕ „			*		
5 62	Chevington .. „			*		

A—Heaton Junction dep. 5.50 a.m., p. 7.   V—Return of No. 2 Down. Trainmen afterwards work No. 92, page 8.

The working timetable commencing 25th September 1938 (although brought in for freight trains on 11th September 1939).

CHEVINGTON and AMBLE—Weekdays

Distance from Chevington	DOWN	1 B Goods	2	3 Light Engine	4 Engine & Van MO Q	6 PASSENGER	7 PASSENGER	8	11 PASSENGER SO	12 PASSENGER SX	13 PASSENGER	14	15 PASSENGER	16 PASSENGER SO	17 PASSENGER SO	18	19 Empty Train SO	20
M.C.		a.m.	a.m.	K a.m.	a.m.	a.m.	a.m.		L p.m.	p.m.	p.m.		p.m.	p.m.	p.m.		p.m.	
.....	**Chevington** .... dep.	—			7 10	9 26	11 31		1 36	2 15	3 33		6 2	7 12	10 5			
0 68	*Amble Junction* ⊕ ,,	—	6 34	6 56	..	..	..		..	..	..		..	..	..		—	
3 28	Broomhill .... ⊕ ,,	6 44	7 40	.....		9 34	11 39		1 44	2 23	3 41		6 10	7 20	10 13		10 54	
5 62	**Amble** .. .. arr.	7 48	—	7 5	7 25	9 41	11 46		1 51	2 30	3 48		6 17	7 27	10 20		11 1	

K—Alnmouth dep. 6.40 a.m., p. 18.
L—Morpeth dep. 1.15 p.m., p. 13.

Distance from Amble	UP	1 B Cattle MO Q	2 PASSENGER	3 D Goods arr.	3 D Goods dep.	4 PASSENGER	5	6 PASSENGER SO	7 PASSENGER SX	8 PASSENGER	9	10	11 PASSENGER	12 PASSENGER	13 Light Engine SX	14 PASSENGER SO	15	16 PASSENGER SO	17 Light Engine SO
M.C.		J a.m.	W a.m.	a.m.	a.m.	a.m.		T p.m.	p.m.	p.m.			p.m.	p.m.	U p.m.	p.m.		p.m.	Y p.m.
.....	**Amble** ... . dep.	6 45	7 42	—	9 0	10 40		12 23	1 30	2 37			5 18	6 27	7 45	8 45		10 40	11 ..
2 34	Broomhill .. ⊕ ,,	..	7 49	9 8	9 45	10 47		12 30	1 37	2 44			5 25	6 34	..	8 52		10 47	..
4 74	*Amble Junction* ⊕ arr.	...	.....	9 55	—	....		...	....	....			....	....	7 55	....		—	11 1
5 62	**Chevington** .. ,,	7 0	7 57	—	—	10 55		12 38	1 45	2 52			5 33	6 42	—	9 0		—	--

J—Runs when there are more than 2 wagons live stock for Newcastle Mart to connect with 5.10 a.m. ex Tweedmouth.
T—Morpeth **arr.** 12.59 p.m., p. 20.
U—Alnmouth **arr.** 8.15 p.m., p. 14.
W—Morpeth **arr.** 8.19 a.m., p. 19.
Y—Alnmouth **arr.** 11.44 p.m., p. 15.

The working timetable for 1st May to 6th July 1930.

CHEVINGTON AND AMBLE BRANCH
WEEKDAYS

Distance from Chevington	DOWN	No.	1305			Distance from Amble	UP	No.	1326	
		Class	K					Class	K	
		Description						Description		
M C			am			M C			am	
.....	**Chevington**		7 40			.....	**Amble**		8 50	
3 28	Broomhill		8a10			2 34	Broomhill		9a15	
5 62	**Amble**		8 18			5 62	**Chevington**		9 25	

No. 1305—Alnmouth 6.5 am, page Q84, **a** arr. 7.50 am   **No. 1326**—**a** Arr. 9.0 am, Alnmouth arr. 1.52 pm, page Q75

The working timetable commencing 10th September 1951.

Locomotives at Broomhill 1947 to 1967 (NCB period)

NCB No	Pre-NCB No	Type	Built	Date allocated		Scrapped
				From	**To**	
	B607 ex-SR	0-6-0T	1876	8/36	1954	1954
	849 *Radcliffe No 3*	0-4-0ST	1899			1947
20	2199 ex-GWR	0-6-0ST	1872	8/36	1955	1955
21	312 ex-GWR	0-6-0T	1907	8/35 1952	1948 1961	April 1961
26		0-6-0T	1945	5/65	9/66	July 1969
28		0-6-0T	1949	8/49 3/62 1965	7/60 7/64 29/3/67	January 1970
32	805 ex-GWR	0-6-0T	1889	8/36	1954	1954
33		0-6-0ST	1945	1945 3/59 7/65 4/66	5/58 12/63 5/65 3/67	March 1973
34	*Blyth*	0-6-0T	1903			February 1962
36		0-6-0T	1943	9/47 6/60 7/64 4/66	7/57 12/63 5/65 3/67	January 1970
51		0-6-0ST	1944	12/63	10/64	February 1970

Amble Customs & Excise and Harbour Master's buildings. (Bartle Rippon)

Amble Railway Station Staff

This list is not complete. The dates refer to the person being at Amble Station in that year. Where given, ages and addresses are as accurate as possible. Names were mainly obtained from Government census records.

Date	Name	Age	Position	Address
1858	Robert King		Station Master	Railway Cottages
1881	Edward Purvis	46	Station Master	Railway Cottages
1901	Frederick Woodward	40	Station Master	Railway Cottages
1903	George Lonsdale		Station Master	Station Cottages
1919	? Wreay		Station Master	Station Cottages
1936	Arthur Bird		Station Master	Station Cottages
1940	Walter Farr		Station Master	Station Cottages
1956	George Waters		Station Master	Station Cottages
1961-69	Frederick Wake		Station Master	Station Cottages
Other Railway Workers				
1858	William Weightman		Employee	
1881	James Purvis	21	Porter	Railway Cottages
1881	William Purvis	16	Clerk	Railway Cottages
1891	Charles Sanderson	25	Railway Fireman	Church Street
	Thomas Matthison	30	Railway Fireman	Church Street
	Joseph Atkinson	54	Guard	Station Cottages
	Robert Stephenson	17	Guard	Leazes Street
	James Reay	44	Carter	Station Cottages
	Michael Elliott	31	Signalman	Railway Cottages
	Joseph Beaty	32	Signalman	Railway Cottages
	Joseph Farrow	37	Signalman	Railway Cottages
	John Wilson	44	Signalman	Station Cottages
	Mark Carr	35	Signalman	Station Cottages
1891	John Lee	14	Clerk	Queen Street
1901	Harold Uoa	19	Clerk	Station Cottages
	James W Wilson	25	Clerk	Station Cottages
	Jacob Bell	33	Clerk	Gordon Street
Post 1901	Richard Byres		Porter	
	William Morton		Platelayer	
	John Mudd		Railway worker	
	Bart Riddle		Platelayer	
	? Topping		Railway worker	

Coal Shipments from Warkworth Harbour, 1909 to 1968
(1st July to 30th June)

Date	Tons	Ships	Date	Tons	Ships
1909/10	446,137	484	1940/41	65,946	48
1910/11	618,361	634	1941/42	59,273	66
1911/12	591,773	621	1942/43	108,977	99
1912/13	629,339	621	1943/44	125,886	110
1913/14	593,339	548	1944/45	98,402	93
1914-18	Not known	Not known	1945/46	112,934	117
1918/19	117,137	145	1946/47	91,430	140
1919/20	206,397	253	1947/48	149,391	312
1920/21	104,558	163	1948/49	161,843	319
1921/22	220,101	206	1949/50	239,199	368
1922/23	358,426	295	1950/51	255,104	382
1923/24	396,650	321	1951/52	330,333	520
1924/25	460,458	333	1952/53	267,385	399
1925/26	404,274	290	1953/54	353,884	515
1926/27	282,806	248	1954/55	357,994	509
1927/28	469,583	377	1955/56	331,581	485
1928/29	552,345	425	1956/57	289,851	396
1929/30	601,167	439	1957/58	215,993	353
1930/31	476,260	342	1958/59	242,017	385
1931/32	441,475	313	1959/60	114,008	229
1932/33	454,657	327	1960/61	125,776	247
1933/34	436,919	299	1961/62	141,891	271
1934/35	424,259	315	1962/63	203,885	378
1935/36	409,872	306	1963/64	316,006	495
1936/37	381,237	322	1964/65	263,818	453
1937/38	333,596	266	1965/66	200,747	355
1938/39	281,626	255	1966/67	185,964	292
1939/40	212,212	164	1967/68	Not known	Not known
Total 1909-40	10,904,964	9,312	Total 1940-68	5,409,518	8336

Total 1909 to 1968	Total Tonnage: 16,323,794	Total Ships: 17,648